THE
TEDDY
BEAR
CRAFT
BOOK

Gyles Brandreth, wearing one of his favourite jumpers and holding three of his favourite bears from the Teddy Bear Museum collection: Steiff bears from 1903, 1905 and 1906.

THE
TEDDY
BEAR
CRAFT
BOOK

FOREWORD BY
GYLES BRANDRETH

CHARLES LETTS · *Letts*® · FOUNDED 1796

© copyright Complete Editions 1991

Editor: Sandy Ransford
Designer: Craig Dodd
Illustrations: Sara Sliwinska, Sergio Ransford
Knitting grids: Clive Sutherland
Photography: Julie Fisher
Stylist: Simon Lycett

First published in 1991
by Charles Letts & Co Ltd
Diary House, Borough Road,
London SE1 1DW

A CIP catalogue record for this book
is available from the British Library
ISBN 1 85238 127 2

'Letts' is a registered trademark of Charles Letts (Scotland) Ltd

Printed and bound in Singapore

Contents

Contributors

The items featured in this book were designed and made by
the following people:

✽ Sue Chappell, Vivienne Hall, Anne Heathcote, Anita Jackson:
  Padded Teddy Suit, page 68.
✽ Patricia de Menezes:
  Child's Brooch, page 86; Bear Up a Stick, page 86; Card Toys, page 86.
✽ Jacqui Hine:
  Tea Party Cake, page 48; Bear Family Biscuits, page 53; Chocolate Teddies, page 56;
  Marzipan Bears, page 58; Christening Plaques, page 61.
✽ Joyce Luckin:
  Jamie Bear, page 11; Benjamin Bear, page 16; Benjamin's Rambler Outfit, page 19;
  Benjamin's Artist Outfit, page 22; Benjamin's Chef Outfit, page 24; Bedtime Benjamin, page 27;
  Beehive Tea-cosy, page 80; Teddy Egg-cosy, page 46; Teatime Traycloth, page 64; Honey Pot Cover, page 66
  Pyjama Case, page 82; Moneybags Bear, page 77; Teddy Motifs, page 67.
✽ Simon Lycett, Bridget Jones:
  Bears to Bake, page 62.
✽ Linda O'Brien:
  Greedy Bear, page 30; Family Bears, page 36;
  Swinging Bear, page 41; Teddy Mittens, page 44.
✽ Sergio Ransford:
  Teddy's Train, page 106.
✽ Petronella Rasmussen:
  Teddies in Print, page 88; Teddy Bookmark, page 93; Sky-diving Bears Mobile, page 94;
  Teddy's Adventure Cards, page 98; Pop-up Birthday Teddy, page 102.
✽ Valerie Tyler:
  Teddy Bear Sampler, page 74.

An unusual teddy bear purse, c.1913.

Foreword

I have been collecting teddy bears ever since I was three. I am sorry to have to admit that this means I have been an ardent arctophile for some forty years. I am happier to reveal that eventually I had collected so many that I had to open a museum in which to house them. At the national Teddy Bear Museum in Stratford-upon-Avon we celebrate every aspect of the teddy bear, from his arrival just after the turn of the century to his worldwide popularity today. In Shakespeare's time the wonderful Elizabethan building – which despite now being known as 19 Greenhill Street still boasts its original oak beams – was a farmhouse. Today it is the home of several hundred teddy bears from over twenty-five different countries around the world. Many of the bears on display come from the private collection that I have built up with my wife Michèle over the years. Many have been loaned or generously donated to the museum by their owners or creators. All of them have distinct individual personalities – and that is the remarkable phenomenon of the teddy bear. Even if two bears are made to the same pattern, those two bears will assume their own unique personalities the moment they have been made. I know that sounds improbable, but it's true. It's also something that you probably knew already or you wouldn't be reading a copy of *The Teddy Bear Craft Book*.

Did you know that the teddy bear owes his name to President Theodore 'Teddy' Roosevelt, twenty-fifth President of the United States? On 14 November 1902 Roosevelt was on a hunting expedition in Smedes, Mississippi. Anxious that the President bag a bear, some of his party chased down and stunned a 107 kg (235 lb) black bear. The hunters roped the animal and tied it to a tree. A messenger was despatched to summon the President so that he might shoot the bear and go home with a trophy. When Roosevelt arrived, he declined to shoot the tethered creature and declared, 'Spare the bear!' The next day *The Washington Post* informed the nation: 'President called after the beast had been lassoed, but he refused to make an unsportsmanlike shot.' The cartoonist Clifford Berryman immortalized the moment in a drawing for *The Washington Post*. Soon after this incident the President was approached by Morris Michtom, a shopkeeper from Brooklyn, who sought presidential permission to manufacture a small toy bear-cub and be allowed to call it 'Teddy's Bear'.

If the teddy bear got his name in the United States, where did he originate from? Germany credits the invention of the teddy bear to the Steiff company, which was begun at Giengen in Swabia in 1880 by a crippled seamstress, Margarete Steiff. The business began as a home workshop producing felt elephants, but by 1902 Steiff were manufacturing a wide range of soft toys, including cats, dogs, pigs, donkeys, horses and camels, but not, until 1903, a bear. When teddy bears are sold at auction today, it is invariably the early Steiff bears that fetch the highest prices.

In my book every bear is priceless. Naturally I treasure the old Steiff bears in my collection, but to me the homemade, much-loved modern teddy bear can be quite as precious as the antique that fetches thousands at auction. The world of the teddy bear is an innocent one, a world that 'gives delight and hurts not', a world that appeals to all generations and all nationalities. Now that you have this book in your hands you can create that world for yourself!

Introduction

This is a book for all who love teddy bears, and who wish to create their own special teddy bear world. All the designs are easy to make. Many have been created specially for children, and some children will enjoy making for themselves, possibly with a little help from a grown-up. None of the designs requires specialized knowledge of any craft featured, which include sewing and embroidery, knitting, cooking, paper work and simple printing techniques.

Each design is illustrated with a full colour photograph, and most also have accompanying colour artwork explaining techniques and the order of work to follow. Where possible, these illustrations are reproduced in the same size as the object to be created, but sometimes they have had to be reduced in size. Where this occurs most have a grid overlay in which 1 cm of the grid equals 2 cm of the real size – that is, they are reproduced half size. In order to create your own, full-size design, draw a grid with 2 cm squares and very carefully, square by square, transfer the design from the book on to it. When making items in fur fabric, such as the toy bears and purse, make sure you also transfer the arrows showing the direction of the pile on the fabric.

The knitting projects which feature motifs each have a grid of small squares in which each square equals one stitch. They are reproduced in full colour, too, so it is easy to see which stitch you have arrived at and what colour it should be.

Each project has a list of necessary materials and equipment, most of which can be found in the average home or bought from a local craft shop. Happy bear making!

CLASSIC
BEARS

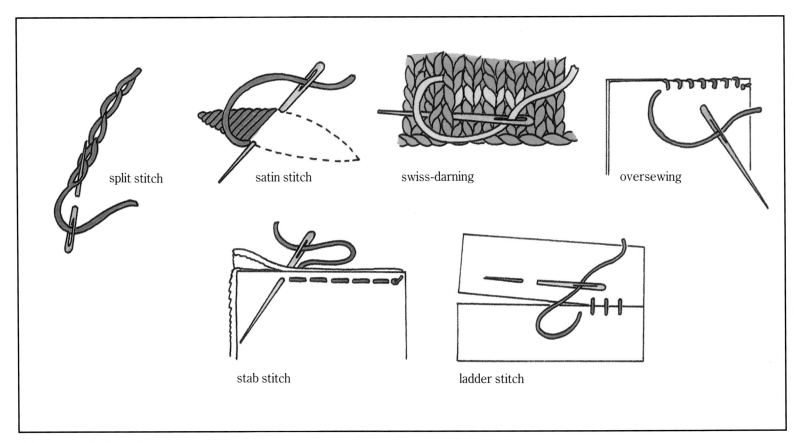

split stitch satin stitch swiss-darning oversewing

stab stitch ladder stitch

Stitches used in the projects.

Jamie Bear is 25cm/10in high and was specially made for a two-year-old friend called James. The bear was designed to be just the right size for little hands and he has been a firm favourite ever since.

Materials

45cm/18in square of fur fabric
1 pair of 10mm/½in safety
   eyes
Small pieces of felt or suede
   for pads and paws
Black wool for nose and
   mouth
Approximately 600g/20oz
   polyester stuffing
45cm of 10mm wide/18in of
   ½in wide ribbon for neck
Small ball of double knitting
   wool (any colour) for jersey
Pair 4mm/no. 8 needles
Length of contrasting wool (to
   match neck ribbon) for
   jersey motif
5 30mm/1¼in joints, with a
   cotter pin

Please read before making

Always cut fur fabric on the wrong side using the points of the scissors only, to prevent the pile being cut away. The arrows on the diagrams show the direction of the pile. Remember to cut one in reverse wherever two pieces are to be cut. Before joining, pin, tack and sew. This is important because fabric with a pile will move when working. The size of the bear will vary a little according to the length of the pile you use and the turnings you take on the seams. Use a stab stitch throughout; that is, putting the needle in one side and back from the other in two separate movements keeping the stitches close together (see page 10). When putting right sides of fur fabric together, stroke the pile away from the seam with a sewing needle.

Method

1. Cut out all the shapes shown in the diagram in fur fabric. The pile should stroke flat in the direction of the arrows.
2. Stitch the leg seams and sew in the pad matching A and B as marked on sole and leg patterns. Leave opening for stuffing where marked.
3. Sew paws on inner arms matching E and F where marked.
4. Sew seams, leaving opening where marked for stuffing.
5. Stitch round the body, G(a) to G, H to I and on to J. The opening G to H is for stuffing the body.
6. Insert gusset in head, matching C to C and D to D. Pin into position before sewing, and snip where indicated by the dotted lines for the insertion of the ears.

7. Stitch round the curved edges of the ears on the wrong side and then turn right side out.
8. Put in the ears in the spaces left and sew carefully to get them nicely positioned. This operation needs special care.
9. Fix the safety eyes where shown, or position them to suit yourself. Do not put them too high in the head or too wide apart. It is a good idea to put a little circle of black or brown felt immediately behind each eye before inserting them into the head, and another piece on the inside before fixing the back of the button. This gives a good appearance to the eyes and fixes them more firmly in the head.
10. With black darning wool sew on the nose and mouth as shown.
11. With the ears, eyes and nose in position, stuff the head firmly. ▷

Pattern pieces. 1cm on the grid ▷ equals 2cm.

stitch line

HEAD

cut 2, 1 in reverse

o

d

c

EAR

cut 4

c

HEAD GUSSET

cut 1

d

Motif for sweater. Sew in eyes, nose and mouth with black darning wool.

j

ga

g

BODY

cut 2, 1 in reverse

h

i

PAW

cut 2 in felt or suede, 1 in reverse

e e

f f

UNDER ARM

cut 2, 1 in reverse

OUTER ARM

cut 2, 1 in reverse

a **PAD** b

cut 2 in felt or suede

LEG

cut 2, 1 in reverse

a b

LEG

cut 2, 1 in reverse

b a

→ direction of pile

cotter pin

fur fabric

washer

CROWN JOINT

NOSE
stitch downwards

▷ 12. Put the joint in the head with the shaft sticking out, gather round the open edge with thread, draw it up tightly and fasten off. It is a good idea to go round a second time to keep it firmly in position.

13. With the body still unstuffed, gather the top of it in the same way. Put a disc in position then snap in the disc that fastens the joint, or make a crown joint (see diagram) if you are using joints with cotter pins.

14. Turn the legs right side out and stuff them firmly, making sure each foot is a good shape. Put the joint into the leg with the shaft sticking out. Oversew round the open edge and secure using thread or double cotton. Repeat for second leg. Make sure both legs have the shaft of the joint facing inwards.

15. Turn the arms right side out and place each joint into position with the shaft facing out. Stuff firmly and oversew the openings using strong thread or double cotton. Make sure the shafts are sticking out on the inner arms where the paws are.

16. Now you have the head, legs and arms firmly fixed and ready to attach to the body. Note the position on the pattern, and when pushing the shaft through the body place a piece of felt inside before putting on the disc and the final fixing disc. Make sure it is very firm.

17. Stuff the body and oversew the opening using thread or double cotton.

18. Using the blunt end of a needle, prise out any fur which has got stuck in the seams.

19. Now knit Jamie's jersey.

Knitted Jersey

Using 4mm needles cast on 30 sts.
K1, P1 for 4 rows.
K1 row, P1 row (stocking st) for 16 rows.
With right side facing, cast on 10 sts and K to end of row.
With wrong side facing, cast on 10 sts and K2, P46, K2 to end of row. This gives a neat edge to the sleeve.
Continue in stocking st on these 50 sts for 13 rows.
With wrong side facing, K2, P8, K30, P8, K2.
K across all 50 sts.
With wrong side facing, K2, P8, K30, P8, K2.
K across all 50 sts.
Cast off. Make another piece exactly the same and sew shoulder seams, underarm and side seams.
Use a Swiss darning st to embroider the teddy motif on the jersey, as shown.

Jamie in his knitted jersey. ▷

Benjamin Bear

Benjamin Bear is approximately 35cm/14in high.

Materials

Approximately ½ metre/
½ yard fur fabric
5 3cm/1½in joints
1 pair of 2cm/1in safety eyes
Small pieces of felt or suede
    for soles and paws
Button thread or Sylko (used
    double)
Black embroidery thread
Approximately 1 kilo/2lbs
    polyester stuffing

Please read before making

Always cut fur fabric on the wrong side using the points of the scissors only, to prevent the pile being cut away. The arrows on the diagrams show the direction of the pile. Remember to cut one in reverse wherever two pieces are to be cut. Before joining, pin, tack and sew. This is important because fabric with a pile will move when working. The size of the bear will vary a little according to the length of the pile you use and the turnings you take on the seams. Use a stab stitch throughout; that is, putting the needle in one side and back from the other in two separate movements keeping the stitches close together (see page 10). When putting right sides of fur fabric together, stroke the pile away from the seam with a sewing needle.

Method

1. Cut out all the pattern pieces as follows.
2. Cut two pieces of head pattern in fur fabric. The pile should stroke flat in the direction of the arrows. Then cut one head gusset and match up D to D and E to E. Stitch as marked.
3. Cut two pieces of body pattern and one piece of body gusset. Put A to A (gusset to body) and match round to C. Stitch.
4. Cut out four pieces of leg pattern and stitch as marked, leaving the opening where shown. Cut out two soles in suede or felt and sew into the leg, matching G to F.
5. Cut out two outer arms and two under arms. Cut out two paws in suede or felt to match the soles. Then sew the paws on to the under arms. Stitch the outer and under arms together as shown, leaving the opening.
6. Cut four ears and stitch them together in pairs as shown by the dotted line. Turn the pieces right side out and go back to the head.
7. Pin the ears to the head to get the sort of expression that you like. Towards the top of the head gives a surprised look, lower down, a laid-back look. When you are satisfied, sew them in position.
8. Check the position of the eyes to get the look you want, then fix them in place. Do not put them too high in the head. Embroider the nose and mouth with black embroidery cotton or wool, then stuff the head firmly.
9. Place the joint (spike sticking downwards) into the head. Sew with running stitches round the neck opening, pull it up and fasten off firmly. Put the spike from the head joint into the body, put on the washer and then fasten and fix firmly.
10. Place the joints in the arms where shown by the dot on the pattern and place into the body, also shown by a dot on the pattern. Put on the washer and then fix firmly.
11. Do the same with the legs.
12. You now have a bear with a head, a floppy body and limbs. Stuff the limbs firmly, fastening the opening with double cotton and overstitching. Stuff the body firmly and overstitch the opening.

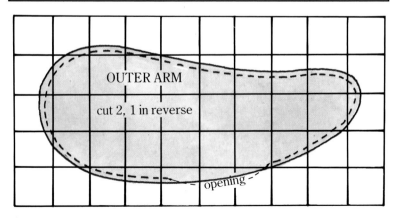

OUTER ARM

cut 2, 1 in reverse

opening

Pattern pieces. 1cm on the grid equals 2cm.

nose

mouth

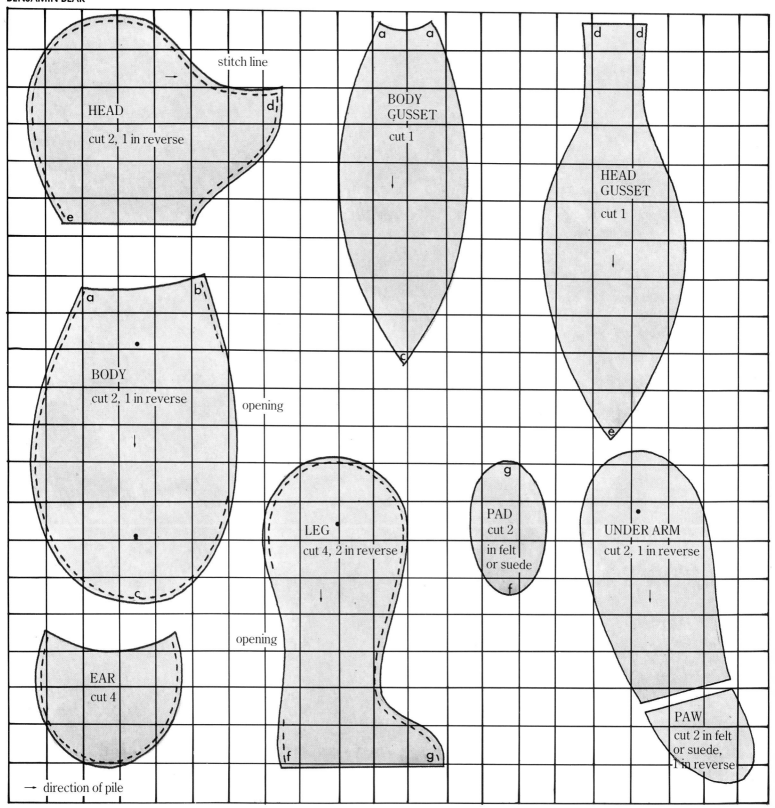

stitch line

HEAD

cut 2, 1 in reverse

BODY
GUSSET

cut 1

HEAD
GUSSET

cut 1

BODY

cut 2, 1 in reverse

opening

LEG

cut 4, 2 in reverse

PAD
cut 2

in felt
or suede

UNDER ARM

cut 2, 1 in reverse

opening

EAR

cut 4

PAW

cut 2 in felt
or suede,
1 in reverse

→ direction of pile

In his thick green sweater, yellow knitted hat and stout rucksack with its teddy bear motif, Benjamin Bear is ready to face all emergencies.

Materials

50g/1½oz green double knitting yarn (or colour of your choice)
25g/¾oz buttercup yellow double knitting yarn (or colour of your choice)
Pair 2¾mm/no. 12 knitting needles
Pair 3mm/no. 11 knitting needles
Blue denim
Small piece of card
0.75 metre/2ft 6in blue tape
Scrap of orange or brown felt

Sweater

In green double knitting yarn with 2¾mm needles cast on 50 sts.
K1, P1 for 10 rows.
Change to 3mm needles.
K1 row, P1 row (stocking st) for 36 rows.
K10, cast off 30, K10.
P10, cast on 30, P10.
K1 row, P1 row for 36 rows.
Change to 2¾mm needles.
K1, P1 for 10 rows, cast off.
Pick up 30 sts with 2¾mm needles round the neck of jumper in the front and K1, P1 along the row.
Continue for 6 rows, cast off.
Repeat for back of neck. Sew shoulders seams.

Sleeves

Cast on 30 sts with 2¾mm needles.
K1, P1 for 10 rows.
Change to 3mm needles.
K1 row, P1 row for 28 rows, cast off.
Repeat for second sleeve.
Sew up underarm seams.
Sew sleeves into sweater and sew up side seams.

Hat

In yellow double knitting yarn and 3mm needles cast on 80 sts.
K1, P1 along the row for 15 rows.
K1 row, P1 row for 12 rows.
*K10 sts, K2 tog., continue from * along the row.
Continue in stocking stitch for 9 rows.
*K9, K2 tog., continue from * along the row.
Continue in stocking stitch for 7 rows.
*K8, K2 tog., continue from * along the row.
Continue in stocking stitch for 5 rows.
*K7, K2 tog., continue from * along the row.
Continue in stocking stitch for 3 rows.
*K6, K2 tog., continue from * along the row.
K1 row stocking stitch and then draw all the stitches up on one thread and fasten off.
Sew up seam. Make a pom-pom by winding yarn round thumb and forefinger about 20 times. Wind yarn round middle of the yarn ball. Secure with a sewing needle and sew on to top of hat. Cut other edges to form a pom-pom.

Rucksack

1. Cut a strip of blue denim 30cm/12in × 12cm/4½in and four strips of 12cm/4½in × 2cm/¾in.
2. Divide the material for the bag into a 10cm/4in flap, half of which is doubled under, a front piece of 7cm/2¾in, a bottom of 2cm/¾in and a back of 7cm/2¾in (see diagram 1). Sew a narrow strip to the back, front and bottom of the bag (diagram 2).
3. Trace off the bear pattern shown, cut it out in felt and stitch it on the flap.
4. Fold the back and the front of the bag together, A - B, and sew the strip together on the wrong side. Neaten the bottom by turning in, and mitre the corner at C. Repeat on the other side.
5. Flatten out the bottom of the bag and line it with a piece of thin card measuring approximately 11cm/4in by 2cm/¾in.
6. Measure matching tape to fit round the top of the arms of Benjamin Bear and sew to the top of the bag on the back, as shown in diagram 3.

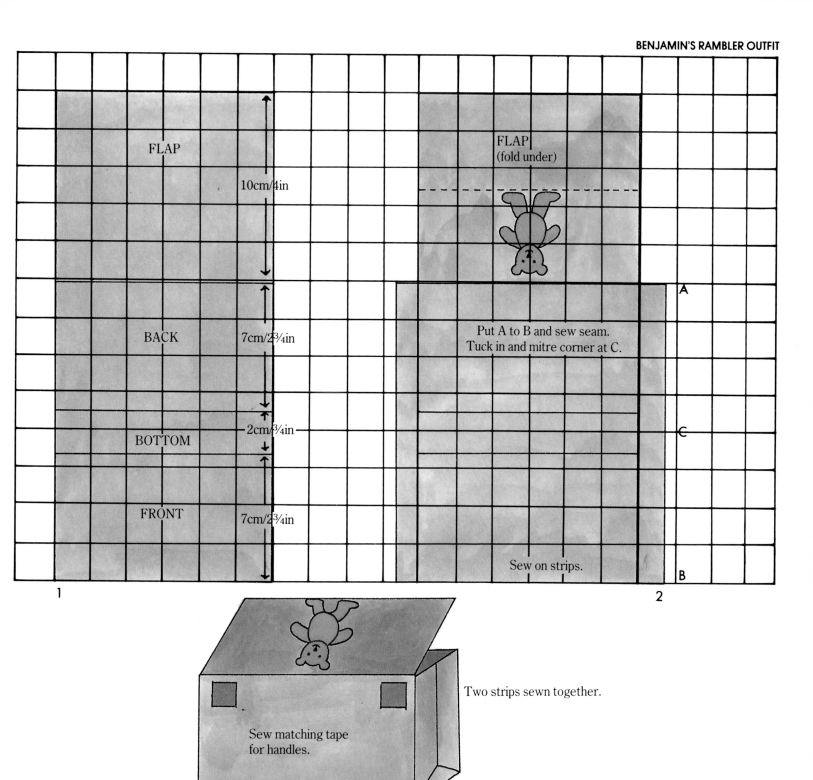

FLAP

FLAP
(fold under)

10cm/4in

BACK

7cm/2¾in

Put A to B and sew seam.
Tuck in and mitre corner at C.

A

BOTTOM

2cm/¾in

C

FRONT

7cm/2¾in

Sew on strips.

B

1

2

Two strips sewn together.

Sew matching tape
for handles.

3

Mitred corner.

*Pattern for rucksack
1cm on the grid equals 2cm.*

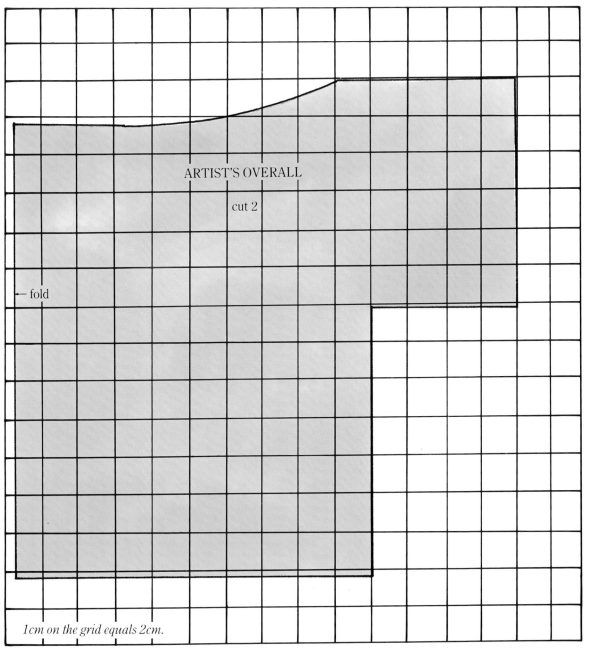

ARTIST'S OVERALL

cut 2

← fold

1cm on the grid equals 2cm.

Here is Benjamin Bear in creative mood.

Overall

1. Cut two pieces from pattern A in the oatmeal material.
2. Sew the underarm and side seams, then turn up and sew a 2cm/¾in hem.
3. Hem 2cm/¾in at the end of the sleeve.
4. Sew a 2cm/¾in seam round the neck. Insert the elastic and draw it up to fit snugly round the bear's neck.

Hat

1. Cut out a 40cm/16in diameter circle of red material, and sew a 2cm/¾in hem round the edge.
2. Put in the elastic and draw it up to fit the head of the bear, then fasten off.
3. Cut out a palette in card, cut down the handle of an ordinary paintbrush, and Benjamin is ready to be creative.

Benjamin's Chef Outfit

Here's Benjamin dressed ready to try out his favourite recipes.

Materials

Approximately 30cm × 40cm/12in × 16in blue cotton material

3 metres/4ft × 3cm/1in wide white tape

40cm × 20cm/16in × 8in strip and a 20cm/16in diameter circle of white cotton material

9cm × 40cm/4in × 16in interfacing

Apron

1. Cut out the apron pattern in blue cotton, and make a 2cm/¾in hem on three sides i.e. the sides and top.
2. Make a 3cm/1in hem at the bottom.
3. Sew the white tape from side to side of the apron 5cm/2in from the bottom of the hem, folding it round the side hems and fastening it off neatly.
4. Sew another strip from side to side just below the curve for the arm, about 5cm/2in from the other strip. Leave about 14cm/5½in on each side for tying. Neaten the ends of the tape with a small hem.
5. Sew another strip 5cm/2in from the second strip and turn over the armhole hem and neaten.
6. Sew neck tapes at the top of the apron, leaving 12cm/4½in each side for tying at the back of neck. Neaten the tape ends with a small hem.

Hat

1. Take the strip of white material 20cm/8in wide and 40cm/16in long, fold it in half widthways and place a piece of interfacing 9cm × 40cm/4in × 16in inside it. Sew a side seam after adjusting the band to fit the head of the bear.
2. Take the circle of white material, gather right round the outside edge and pull it up to fit the top edge of the band.
3. Pin it to the inside of the band and sew on the wrong side. Fold under the edge of the outside of the band and sew it to the gathered top of the hat.
4. Add a small wooden spoon and Benjamin Bear is ready to tackle that recipe.

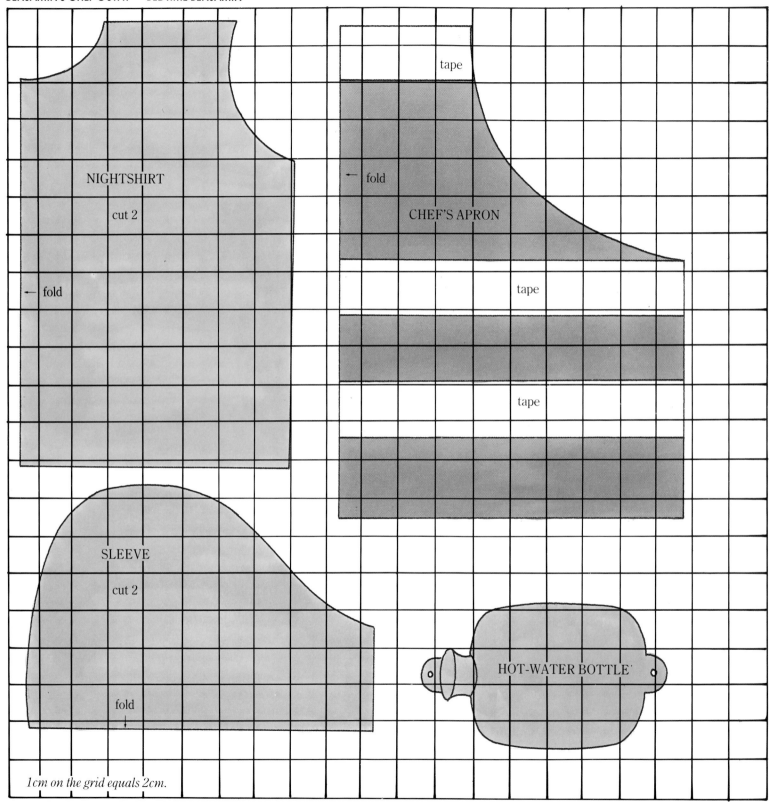

NIGHTSHIRT

cut 2

← fold

CHEF'S APRON

← fold

tape

tape

tape

SLEEVE

cut 2

fold

HOT-WATER BOTTLE

1cm on the grid equals 2cm.

Bedtime Benjamin

After all his activity, Benjamin Bear is tired, so he is hopping into his night attire and has filled his hot-water bottle ready for bed.

Materials

½ metre/½ yard striped material
4 small matching buttons
Small piece of elastic
2 press-studs
25 grams/¾oz double knitting wool for knitted cap
Pink felt for hot-water bottle

Nightshirt

1. Cut out two pieces of nightshirt pattern in the striped material. Cut on the cross a strip of material approximately 3cm/1in wide, and cut two pieces of the sleeve pattern.
2. Join the shoulder seams.
3. Sew the top of the sleeve into the front and back of the nightshirt after gathering the top of the sleeve slightly to ease it into the armhole. Sew the side seams of the shirt and sleeve.
4. Make a 1cm/½in hem at the bottom of the nightshirt.
5. Cut the front opening about 13cm/5in long, bind the neck edge and the underneath of the front opening.
6. Cut on the cross a strip of material 3cm × 15cm/1in × 6in. Face the uppermost front opening with this material. Place the strip on the front of the nightshirt, right sides together and with the raw edges aligned. Stitch about 1cm/½in from the edge. Fold the facing round the edge of the nightshirt, turn under the raw edge and hem it to the under side, within the line of your first stitching.
7. Sew on buttons on the uppermost front opening.
8. Sew two press-studs under the top two buttons for fastening the nightshirt.
9. Make a 2cm/1in hem at the edge of the sleeve and press into a turn-back cuff if desired.
10. To make a neater fit, put a little elastic in the binding at the back of the neck and secure at both ends.

Hot-water Bottle

1. Cut two pieces of the hot-water bottle shape in pink felt, or colour of your choice. Oversew round the outside edge, leaving a small opening.
2. Put a little stuffing in the opening to pad out the bottle, then finish the oversewing.
3. Make a small hole in the top flap and thread a piece of cotton through it for holding the hot-water bottle.

Hat

1. Make a nightcap in red or white wool to the pattern given in the Rambler outfit. Benjamin Bear is now ready for bed.

Overleaf: Bedtime Benjamin.

WOOLLY
BEARS

30

Materials

4 50g balls of double knitting
    yarn in 1st colour, **sky
    blue** (B)
3 balls in 2nd colour, **dark
    green** (D)
2 balls in 3rd colour, **light
    brown** (A)
1 ball in each of 4 other
    colours, **dark brown** (C),
    peach (E), **red** (F), **apple
    green** (G)
A small amount of **white** (H)
1 pair each of 3¼mm/no. 10
    and 4mm/no. 8 needles
3 stitch-holders

*The quantities of yarn given
are based on average
requirements and are therefore
approximate.*

Knitting needle size equivalents

Metric mm	British	American
2.75	12	2
3.00	11	3
3.25	10	4
3.75	9	5
4.00	8	6

Measurements

To fit bust/chest: 96 (101:107) cm
(38 (40:42) in).
Actual measurement: 106
(111:117) cm (42 (44¼:46½) in).
Length from shoulder: 63cm
(25in).
Sleeve length: 48cm (19in).
*Figures in brackets refer to the
larger sizes. Where only one figure
is given this refers to all sizes.*

Tension

22 sts and 28 rows to 10cm (4in)
on 4mm needles over st.st.

Abbreviations

K = knit; P = purl; st(s) =
stitch(es); st.st. = stocking
stitch; beg. = beginning; foll.
= following; inc. = increase;
dec. = decrease; cont. =
continue; RS = right side; WS
= wrong side; rep = repeat;
rem. = remaining; cm =
centimetre; in = inch; patt. =
pattern.

Method

Back
With 3¼mm needles and A, cast
on 98 (104:110) sts and work in
K1, P1, rib for 20 rows.
Change to 4mm needles.
Increase row: K6 (9-12), inc. in
next st * K4 inc. in next st, rep.
from * to last 6 (9-12) sts, K to
end of row. (116(122-128) sts).
Next row: P.**

Place chart
Now starting with the 1st row,
work from **back** chart, using
separate balls of yarn for each
colour block, winding yarn around
each other at colour changes on
every row to stop a hole forming.
Work between appropriate lines
for size required. *Do not work* sts
denoted as / which will be
swiss-darned when work is
completed. Work these sts in
background colour for that area.
Cont. straight as set until 150
rows of chart have been worked,
thus ending with a WS row.

Shape back neck
Next row: (151st row of chart)
Patt. 43 (46-49) sts, turn and
cont. on this first set of sts only,
placing rem. sts on a stitch-holder.
***Dec., 1 st at neck edge on
next 3 rows.
Cast off rem. 40 (43:46) sts fairly
loosely. (154 rows of chart
complete.)
Return to rem. sts. and slip first
30 sts on to stitch-holder. With RS
facing rejoin appropriate yarn to
rem. sts and patt. to end of row.
Now work as for first side from
*** to end.

▷

Front chart.

/ = swiss-darning

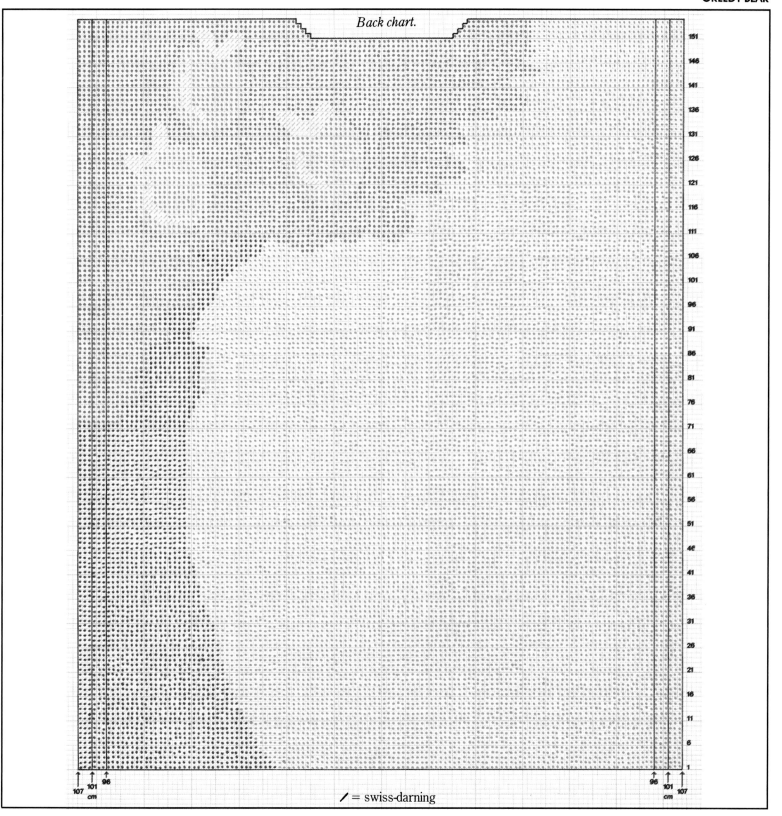

Back chart.

/ = swiss-darning

▷ Front

Work as for back to **.

Place chart

Now starting with the 1st row, work from **front** chart, using separate balls of yarn for each colour block, winding yarn around each other at colour changes on every row to stop a hole forming. Work between appropriate lines for size required. *Do not work* sts denoted as /, which will be swiss-darned when work is completed. Work these sts in background colour for that area. Cont. straight as set until 136 rows of chart have been worked, thus ending with a WS row.

Shape front neck

Next row: (137th row of chart) Patt. 50 (53:56) sts, turn and cont. on this first set of sts only, placing rem. sts on a stitch-holder. **** Keeping chart correct, dec. 1 st at neck edge on every row until 40 (43:46) sts remain. Now cont. straight until chart is complete. (154 rows of chart complete.) Cast off all sts fairly loosely. Return to rem. sts and slip first 16 sts on to stitch-holder. With RS facing rejoin appropriate yarn to rem. sts and patt. to end of row. Now work as for first side from **** to end.

First sleeve

With 3¼mm needles and B, cast on 46 sts and work in K1, P1, for 20 rows.
Change to 4mm needles.
Increase row: *K1, inc. in next st rep. from * to last 2 sts K. to end. (68 sts).
Now starting with a P row work in st. st., but at the same time, inc. 1 st at each end of every foll. 6th row until there are 106 sts on the needle.
Now work straight in st. st. until sleeve measures 48 cm from cast-on edge, ending with a WS row.
Cast off fairly loosely.

Second sleeve

Work as for first sleeve, but using colour D throughout.

Neckband

Join right shoulder.
With 3¼mm needles and D and RS facing, pick up and K 21 sts down left front neck, K 16 sts from front stitch-holder, pick up and K 21 sts up right front neck, K 4 sts down right back neck, K 30 sts from back stitch-holder and finally pick up and K 4 sts up left back neck. (96 sts). Work in K1 P1 rib for 20 rows.
Cast off fairly loosely ribwise.

To make up

Work swiss-darning in colours as shown on charts.
Press according to ball-band instructions.
Join left shoulder and neckband seam.
Fold neckband in half to inside and slipstitch loosely in position.
Measure and mark 25cm each side of shoulder seam and sew sleeves between these marks.
Join side and sleeve seams.

Swiss-darning

1. Working from the back, insert the needle at the bottom of the stitch to be covered and pull the yarn through to the front.
2. Pass the needle from right to left under the two loops of the same stitch one row above and bring the yarn or thread through to the front.
3. Re-insert the needle into the base of the original stitch.
4. Continue working in this manner, taking care to keep the stitches at the same tension as the knitting.
5. At the end of the row insert the needle into the base of the last stitch worked and up through the centre of the same stitch.
6. Insert the needle from left to right under the two loops of this stitch on the row above and continue working along the row.

Back of Greedy Bear jumper. ▷

Materials

6 (7:7) 50g balls of double knitting yarn in 1st colour, **sky blue** (A)
1 ball in each of 5 other colours, **jade** (B), **pink** (C), **brown** (D), **cream** (E), **black** (F)
1 pair each of 3¼mm/no. 10 and 4mm/no. 8 needles
3 stitch-holders
5 buttons

The quantities of yarn given are based on average requirements and are therefore approximate.

Measurements

To fit bust/chest: 66 (71:76) cm (26(28:30) in).
Actual measurement: 75 (80:86) cm (30 (32:34) in).
Length from shoulder: 46 (51:56) cm (18 (20:22) in).
Sleeve length: 40 (43:46) cm (16 (17:18) in).

Tension

22 sts and 28 rows to 10cm (4in) on 4mm needles over st. st.

Abbreviations

K = knit; P = purl; st(s) = stitch(es); st.st. = stocking stitch; beg. = beginning; foll. = following; inc. = increase; dec. = decrease; cont. = continue; RS = right side; WS = wrong side; rep. = repeat; alt. = alternate; rem. = remaining; yfwd = yarn forward; tog. = together; yrn = yarn round needle; yon = yarn over needle; in = inch; cm = centimetre.

Method

Right front
Pocket bag
With 4mm needles and A, cast on 26 sts and starting with a K row, work in st.st for 28 rows. Leave sts on a stitch-holder.

Right front
With 3¼mm needles and A, cast on 35 (38:41) sts and work in K1, P1, rib for 18 rows.
Change to 4mm needles.
Increase row: K2, inc. in next st * K4 inc. in next st. rep. from * to last 7(10-13) sts, K to end of row. (41(44-47) sts).
Next row: P**
St.st. for 2 rows.

Place chart
1st row: K5 (6:7), work across 30 sts from **front** chart in same way as for back, K6 (8:10).
Complete 28 rows of chart thus ending with a WS row.

Pocket opening
With A, K7 (8:9) slip next 26 sts on to a stitch-holder, and with RS facing pick up and K 26 sts from pocket bag, K8 (10:12) to end of row.
Next row: P.
Cont. straight in st.st. for 26 (32:38) rows, thus ending with a WS row.

Front chart for pockets.

/ = swiss-darning

Shape front neck

(Neck edge is at beg. of RS rows on right front and at the end of RS rows on left front.)
Cont. in st.st., dec. 1 st on next and every foll. 3rd row at neck edge until there are 25 (28:31) sts ending with WS row. Work straight for 4 (10:16) rows.
Cast off fairly loosely.

Pocket welt

With 3¼mm needles and F, with RS facing, rejoin yarn to 26 sts on holder and work in K1, P1 rib for 6 rows. Cast off ribwise fairly loosely.

Left front

Work as for Right Front but reverse all shaping.

Back

With 3¼mm needles and A, cast on 70 (76:82) sts and work in K1, P1, rib for 18 rows.
Change to 4mm needles.
Increase row: K7 (10-13), inc. in next st. * K4 inc. in next st, rep. from * to last 7 (10-13) sts, K to end of row. (82 (88-94) sts).
Next row: P**

Place chart

Now starting with the 13th (7th:1st) row, work from **back** chart, using separate balls of yarn for each colour block, winding yarn around each other at colour changes on every row to stop a hole forming.
Work between appropriate lines for size required.
Do not work sts denoted as / which will be swiss-darned when work is completed. Work these sts in background colour for that area.
Cont. straight as set until 116th row of chart has been worked, thus ending with a WS row. Work straight in st.st. for 0(6:12) rows.

Shape back neck

Next row: K28 (31:34) sts, turn and cont. on this first set of sts only, placing rem. sts on a stitch-holder.
***Dec. 1 st at neck edge on next 3 rows.
Cast off rem. 25 (28:31) sts fairly loosely.
Return to rem. sts and slip first 26 sts on to a stitch-holder. With RS facing rejoin appropriate yarn to rem. sts and patt. to end of row. Now work as for first side from *** to end.

Sleeve

With 3¼mm needles and A, cast on 40 sts. and work in K1, P1, for 16 rows.
Change to 4mm needles.
Increase row: K2, inc. in next st, *K1, inc. in next st. rep. from * to last 3 sts K. to end. (58 sts).
Now starting with a P row work in st.st., but at the same time, inc. 1 st at each end of every foll. 6th row until there are 80 (84:86) sts on the needle.
Now work straight in st.st. until sleeve measures 40 (43:46) cm from cast-on edge, ending with a WS row.
Cast off fairly loosely.

Press according to ball-band instructions.
Work swiss-darning in F as shown on charts.
Join both shoulders.

Collar

With 3¼mm needles and E, cast on 13 sts loosely.
1st row: (RS) K9, yfwd, K2 tog., yfwd, K2.
2nd and all alt. rows: yrn. to inc. 1, K2 tog., P to end.
3rd row: K8, (yfwd, K2 tog.) twice, yfwd, K2.
5th row: K7, (yfwd, K2 tog.) 3 times, yfwd, K2.
7th row: K6, (yfwd, K2 tog.) 4 times, yfwd, K2.
9th row: K5, (yfwd, K2 tog.) 5 times, yfwd, K2.
11th row: K5, K2 tog. (yfwd, K2 tog.) 5 times, K1.
13th row: K6, K2 tog. (yfwd, K2 tog.) 4 times, K1.
15th row: K7, K2 tog. (yfwd, K2 tog.) 3 times, K1.
17th row: K8, K2 tog. (yfwd, K2 tog.) twice, K1.
19th row: K9, K2 tog. yfwd, K2 tog., K1.
20th row: yrn. to inc. 1, K2 tog., P to end.
These 20 rows form patt., rep. 11 (12:13) times. Cast off on a 20th row loosely.

Buttonband

With 3¼mm needles and A, cast on 9 sts and work in K1, P1 rib for 4 rows.
Buttonhole row: Rib 4, yon to make 1 st P2 tog. rib 3.
Rib for 17 (19-19) rows.
Rep. last 18 (20-20) rows until there are 5 buttonholes altogether, then cont. in rib until the band fits all around neckline.
Cast off fairly loosely ribwise.

To make up

Using a running stitch gather up straight side of collar to fit neckline from neck shaping.
Position collar centrally and stitch in place.
Now sew buttonband neatly around neck.
Sew pocket bags and welts neatly into position on fronts.
Measure and mark 19 (20:21) cm each side of shoulder seam and sew sleeves between these marks.
Join side and sleeve seams.
Sew on buttons.

Swiss-darning

For instructions on how to do this, see page 10.

Back chart.
/ = swiss-darning

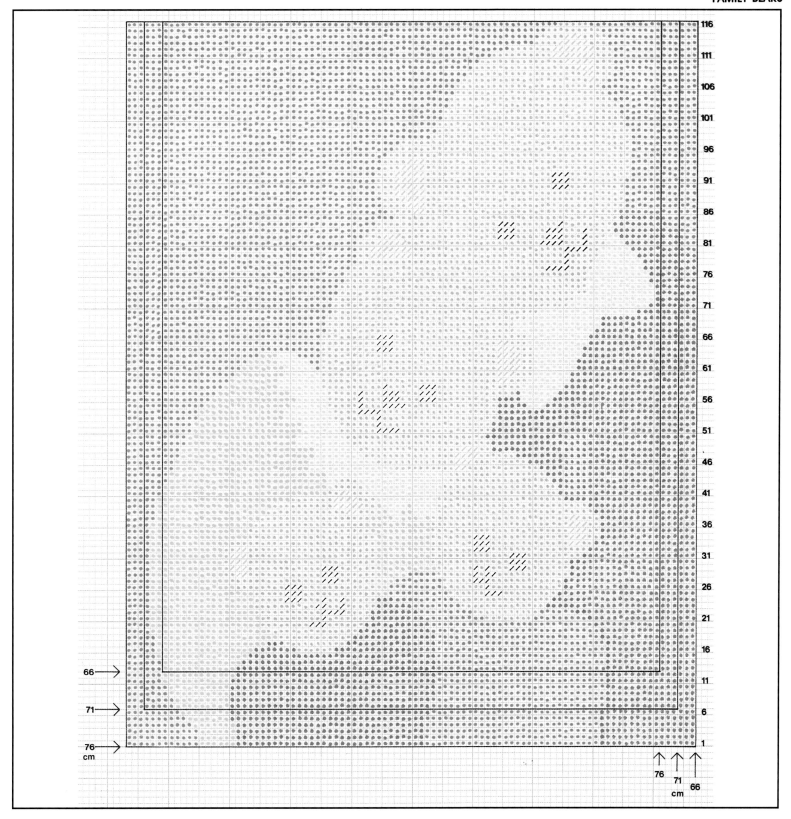

Swinging Bear

Materials

3 50g balls of double knitting yarn in 1st colour, **jade green** (A)
1 ball in each of 3 other colours, **black** (B), **brown** (C), **pink** (D)
1 pair each of 3¼mm (no. 10) and 4mm (no. 8) needles
4 stitch-holders
The quantities of yarn given are based on average requirements and are therefore approximate.

Measurements

Length when worn: approximately 160cm/62in.

Tension

22 sts and 28 rows to 10cm/(4in) on 4mm needles over st. st.

Abbreviations

K = knit; P = purl; st(s) = stitch(es); st.st. = stocking stitch; beg. = beginning; foll. = following; inc. = increase; dec. = decrease; cont. = continue; RS = right side; WS = wrong side; rep. = repeat; rem. = remaining; cm = centimetre; in = inch.

Method

Fingers (Make 4)

With 4mm needles and C, cast on 8 sts and inc. 1 st in each st to end of row (16 sts). Starting with a P row work in st.st. for 17 rows thus ending with a WS row. Leave these sts on stitch-holder.

Scarf

With 3¼mm needles and A, cast on 37 sts and work in K1, P1 rib for 4 rows. Change to 4mm needles and work in st.st. for 36 rows. Change to B and work 4 more rows st.st.

Place chart and fingers as follows
***Next row: With B K9, with C K3, ** with RS of fingers held at front of work against RS of scarf, with C K next st and first st. of finger tog., * K next 2 sts tog. in same way, then pass first st over second st to cast off. Rep. from * 6 times, then leaving 8 sts remaining on holder, K next st on left needle and pass last st over it. (Thus 8 sts have been cast off altogether.) K2, then rep. from ** using second finger, K1, with B K6.

Next row: With B P6, with C P3 then P 8 sts from finger, P3, P 8 sts from next finger, P4, then with B P9.***

Now starting with the first row, work from chart, using separate balls of yarn for each colour block, winding yarn around each other at colour changes on every row to stop a hole forming. *Do not work* sts. denoted as /, which will be swiss-darned when work is completed. Work these sts in background colour for that area. Cont. straight as set until 44 rows of chart have been worked, thus ending with a WS row.

Inc. row: * Inc. in next st, K3, rep. from * to last st., inc. in last st (47 sts).

Next row: * K1.P1.* to last st K. Cont. in single rib until rib measures 120cm ending with a RS row.

Dec. row:* P2 tog., P3 * rep. from * to last 2 sts, P2 tog. (37 sts).

Now turn chart upside-down and work the 44 rows of chart.

Join fingers as before working from *** to ***.

Change to B and work 4 rows st.st.; change to A, and st.st. for 36 rows, then change to 3¼mm needles and work in *K1.P1.* rib for 4 rows. Cast off loosely.

To complete

Work swiss-darning in colours as shown on charts.
Press st.st. areas of scarf according to ball-band instructions.
With a running stitch pull up ends of fingers tightly then stitch up length of finger.
Turn ends of scarf up at finger level and stitch each side up neatly to form a pocket on inside of scarf.

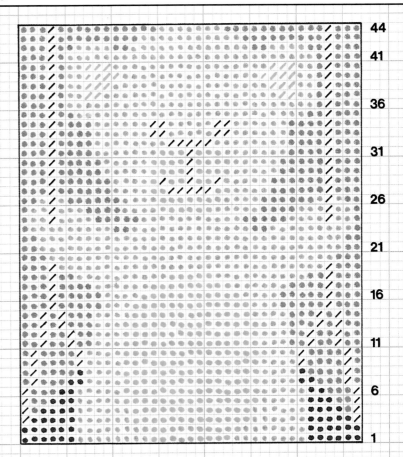

Teddy Mittens

44

These delightful children's mittens, given in two sizes, double as amusing hand puppets.

Materials

1 50g ball of double knitting yarn in each of 2 colours, (A – main colour) and (B – nose and inside mouth colour)

A small amount of 3rd colour (C – tongue colour)

1 pair each of 3¼mm (no. 10) and 4mm (no. 8) knitting needles

2 stitch-holders and a safety pin

Small amounts of white and black felt

The quantities of yarn given are based on average requirements and are therefore approximate.

Measurements

Length of finished glove (including rib): 17(22)cm (7(8½)in)
Width across glove: 7½(9½)cm (3(3¾)in)

Figures in brackets refer to the larger size. When only one size is given this refers to both sizes.

Tension

22 sts and 28 rows to 10cm (4in) on 4mm needles over st.st.

Abbreviations

K = knit; P = purl; st(s) = stitch(es); st.st. = stocking stitch; beg. = beginning; foll. = following; inc. = increase; dec. = decrease; cont. = continue; RS = right side; WS = wrong side; rep. = repeat; rem. = remaining; cm = centimetre; in = inch; SKP = slip one stitch; knit one stitch, then pass slipped stitch over; tog. = together; g st = garter stitch.

Method

Tongue

With 3¼mm needles and C, cast on 3(4)sts and working in g st (knit every row) inc. 1 st at each end of every row until there are 9(12)sts. Work straight for 10(16) rows. Leave these sts on stitch holder.

Mitten

With 3¼mm needles and A, cast on 34(44)sts and work in K1, P1 rib for 13(16)cm.
Change to 4mm needles and work in st.st. for 6(8) rows.
Next row: K15(19), leave last 19(25)sts on holder, turn and P13(16), then leave last 2(3)sts on safety pin.
Working on these sts only, st.st. for 10(12) rows.
Dec. 1 st at each end of next 4 rows.
Change to B, and inc. 1 st at beg. of next 4 rows, then work straight for 10(12) rows.
Cut yarn. Slip 2(3)sts from safety pin back on to needle.

Join tongue

Next row: With B, K2(3)sts (from safety pin), K2, then holding tongue in front of work *K1st from tongue tog. with st from needle, rep. from * across 9(12)sts, K2, then K2(3)sts from stitch-holder, change to A, and K to end of row.
Next row: With A, P17(22), winding yarn around each other, change to B, P17(22).
Cont. in this way as set for 10(12) more rows.

Next row: B K17(22), A K6(8), B K5(6), A K6(8).
Next row: A P5(7), B P7(8), A P5(7), B P17(22).
Next row: B K17(22), A K4(6), B K9(10), A K4(6).
Next row: A P3(5), B P11(12), A P3(5), B P17(22).
Next row: B K17(22), A K2(4), B K13(14), A K2(4).
Next row: A P1(3), B P15(16), A P1(3), B P17(22).

Large size only

Next row: B K22, A K2, B K18, A K2.
Next row: A P1, B P20, A P1, B P22.

All sizes

With B, st.st. for 4 rows.

Shape top

Next row: **SKP, K13(18), K2tog., turn and work on this group of sts only.
Cont. in st.st., dec. 1 st at each end of every row until there are 5(10)sts.
Cast off. Rejoin yarn to rem. sts and work from ** to end.

Ears (make 2)

Work in A exactly as for tongue. Cut yarn and thread end through sts and pull up tightly to form a curved shape and fasten off.

To complete

Stitch up 'thumb' and mitten. Turn rib to inside and slipstitch neatly but not too tightly. Cut out the felt pieces for eyes and nose. Place and stitch on the ears, and the felt eyes and nose securely.
Work second mitten exactly as first.

For large size

White cut 4   EYES   Black cut 4   NOSE Black cut 1

For small size

White cut 4   EYES   Black cut 4   NOSE Black cut 1

Felt shapes for eyes and noses on mittens.

Teddy Egg-cosy

Method

With 2¾mm needles cast on 40 sts.
K1, P1 along the row.
Continue for 6 rows.
Change to 3mm needles.
K1 row, P1 row (stocking st).
Continue for 32 rows.
K2 tog. all along the row.
P1 row.
K9, K into next st (twice), K9.
P1 row.
K9, K into next st, K2, K into next st, K9.
P1 row.
K9, K into next st, K4, K into next st, K9.
P1 row.
K9, K2 tog., K4, K2 tog., K9.
P1 row.
K9, K2 tog., K2, K2 tog., K9.
P1 row.
K9, K2 tog. (twice), K9.
P1 row.
K9, K2 tog., K9.
P1 row.
K4 rows in stocking st and cast off.
Sew top edge and down back of egg-cosy.

Ear

Cast on 2 sts with 3mm needles.
K into next st twice.
K into next st, K2, K into next st.
K into next st, K4, K into next st.
K into next st, K6, K into next st.
K into next st, K8, K into next st.
Cast off. Repeat for second ear.
Gather cast-off edge and sew on both sides of top of head of bear.
Embroider features with black wool.

Arms

Cast on 2 sts with 3mm needles.
K into 1st st, repeat.
P.
K into 1st st, K to end and K into last st.
P.
Cont. until there are 12 sts on the needle.
Cont. in stocking st for 20 rows.
K2 st tog., K to end of row, K2 sts tog.
P.
Cont. decreasing until 2 sts remain. K them tog.
Repeat for second arm.
Sew up seam. Stuff lightly and sew the shaped piece as a shoulder on to the body and fasten hands into position with a stitch.
Stuff head lightly.
Tie bow round the neck.

Materials

Scraps of 4-ply yarn in suitable colours
Pair 2¾mm/no. 12 needles
Pair 3mm/no. 11 needles
Black embroidery wool
Piece of ribbon for neck

BEARS
TO COOK

Tea Party Cake

48

To Assemble the Cake

To Finish the Cake

This cake holds a surprise – it's filled with chocolate teddy bears.

Ingredients

3 cakes cooked in an
   ovenproof pudding basin
   (see page 52)
1kg/2lb chocolate icing
   (see page 52)
750g/1½lb sugarpaste*
  – coloured as follows
175g/7oz white sugarpaste
300g/10oz blue sugarpaste
50g/2oz red sugarpaste
100g/4oz brown sugarpaste
25g/1oz black sugarpaste
Chocolate teddy bears
   (see page 57)
Cake board or tray

*Sugarpaste is also known as 'rolled fondant', and can be bought ready made.

Icing

Slacken the icing with a little milk if necessary to give the right consistency when piped to make soft spreading stars to represent fur.

Body

1. Place two cakes wide side down on the table and slice through each one horizontally twice (step 1).
2. Using a 6cm/2½in cutter, cut out the centres of the four largest slices and reserve these pieces for the legs (step 2).
3. Sandwich each cake back together using a little chocolate icing and fill the centres with wrapped chocolate teddies (see page 57). Trim the cake tops, invert one cake and stick it on top of the other one to make the body (step 3).

Head

1. Slice the remaining cake as for the body but only cut a circle out of the centre slice. Sandwich the cake back together again filling the centre if possible.
2. Trim the head to form the snout and cut away a little cake at the front for the chin and across the base of the head to allow it to sit at a slight angle to the body (step 4). Position the head on the body to check that it is all right, and then remove it.

Legs

1. Stick two reserved circles of cake together for each leg and cut as shown (step 5). Stick the trimmings together with icing and stick into position.
2. Cut the circle from the head cake through the thickness and stick one piece on the end of each leg to make a foot (step 6).
3. Leave the legs detached from the body. Cover all the assembled cake pieces with foil or cling film and leave to 'set' for at least half an hour.

Body

1. Stick the body towards the back of the cake board with a little icing. Trim off a thin slice at the front to leave a little space between the body and the chin.
2. Spread a thin layer of icing all over the body.
3. Place some of the icing in a piping bag fitted with a large star tube or a small potato nozzle.
4. Pipe stars all over the top half of the body to make 'fur'.
5. Divide the sugarpaste into the suggested amounts and colour with coloured food pastes. Do not use liquid colours as they will alter its texture. Coloured food pastes can be bought from cake decorating shops and some delicatessens.
6. Roll out the blue sugarpaste and cut out the trousers. Wrap one piece round the front of the bear and one piece round the back, smoothing the joins at the sides. Measure the length of braces you need and cut out two 1cm/½in wide straps. Stick the trousers and braces into position on the cake.

Fitting the head

If this is difficult to do, secure it in position with a wooden skewer. Remember to remove the skewer before serving.

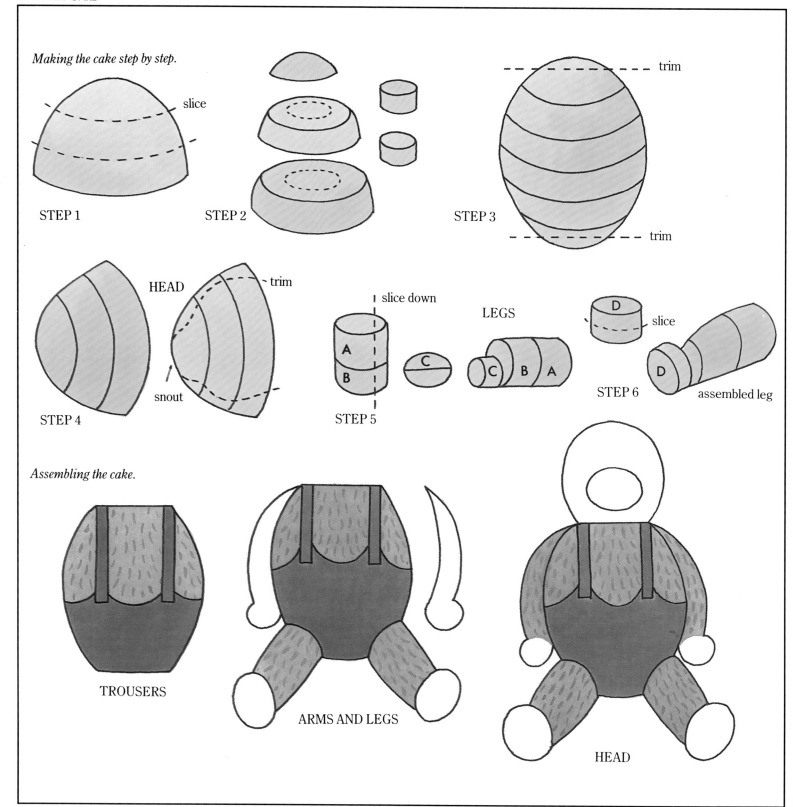

Making the cake step by step.

slice

STEP 1

STEP 2

trim

trim

STEP 3

HEAD

trim

snout

STEP 4

slice down

LEGS

A
B

C

C B A

D

slice

D

STEP 6

assembled leg

STEP 5

Assembling the cake.

TROUSERS

ARMS AND LEGS

HEAD

Legs

1. Slide the legs into position, cover with a thin layer of icing and then pipe icing over them, omitting the soles of the feet.

Arms

1. Reserve small pieces of white sugarpaste for the eyes, buttons and spots on the bow tie, and mould the rest into two arms tapering off at the top and flattened at the bottom for the paws.
2. Position the arms carefully on the cake and pipe icing over them, omitting the paws.

Head

1. Stick the head into position on the body. Cover it carefully with a little icing before piping stars over it.

Ears, Paws, Eyes, Nose and Bow Tie

1. Using 25g/1oz brown sugarpaste for each ear, mould into shape with the fingers. Make a small pleat at the base and push into position on either side of the head. Support them from behind with a cocktail stick and leave to dry for at least half an hour.
2. Use the remaining brown sugarpaste to cut out two paws and two feet and stick into position.
3. Cut out the bow tie from red sugarpaste approximately 76mm/3in long and 26mm/1in wide. Mould into shape.
4. Use the reserved white sugarpaste for the eyes, buttons and spots on the bow tie, and the black sugarpaste for the nose and eyes.
5. Remove the cocktail sticks and carefully pipe icing behind the ears. Place the bow tie in position.

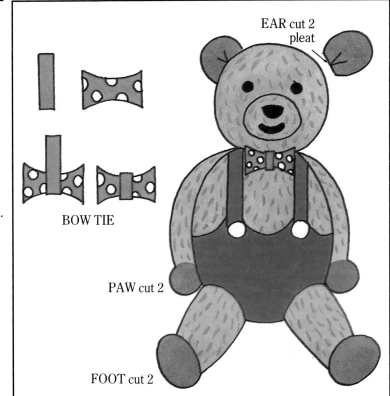

EAR cut 2
pleat

BOW TIE

PAW cut 2

FOOT cut 2

Draw the outline for the trousers by tracing the left side of the pattern, then complete it by reversing the paper and drawing the symmetrical right half.

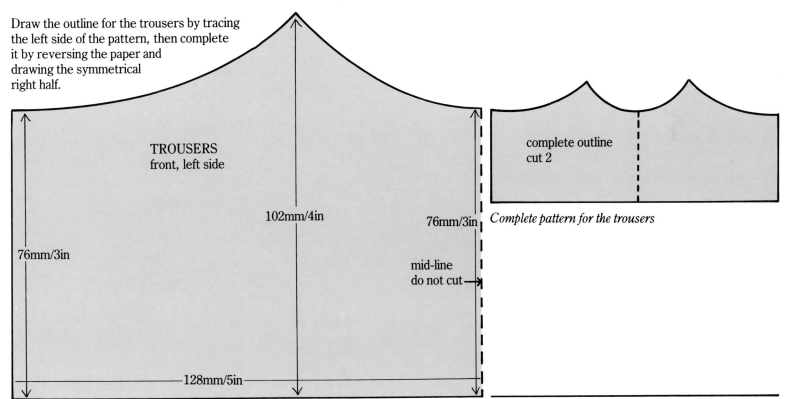

TROUSERS
front, left side

102mm/4in

76mm/3in

76mm/3in

mid-line
do not cut →

128mm/5in

complete outline
cut 2

Complete pattern for the trousers

Basic Recipes

Cake

Basin size 1.25ml/40fl/5 cup.

Ingredients

For each cake
150g/6oz/1½ cups self-raising
    flour
150g/6oz/scant cup
    caster/(superfine) sugar
150g/6oz/¾ cup soft
    margarine
3 eggs
1 tablespoon hot water

Chocolate Icing

Ingredients

500g/1lb/2½ cups butter or
    spread
1kg/2lb/8 cups icing
    (confectioners') sugar
50g/2oz/scant ½ cup drinking
    chocolate powder
Milk

Method

1. Place the butter or spread in a bowl and beat until soft.
2. Sift the icing sugar and chocolate powder together and gradually stir into the butter or spread.
3. Add one or two tablespoons of milk if using butter – a soft spread will not need it – and beat hard for several minutes until the icing is light and fluffy.

Alternatively, place all the ingredients into a food processor or mixer and run the machine, removing the plunger for the last few seconds if possible to allow air to enter the mixture.

A soft spreading butter and vegetable oil mixture may be used in which case a little less milk may be required.

Method

1. Preheat the oven to 180°C/350°F/Gas 4. Grease the basin and place a small circle of greaseproof paper in the base.
2. Place the flour, sugar, margarine, eggs and water in a bowl and beat the ingredients together with an electric mixer for two minutes until the mixture is light and fluffy.
3. Pour the mixture into the prepared basin and level it off.
4. Stand the basin on a baking sheet, and bake in the centre of the oven for twenty minutes, then reduce the oven temperature to 160°C/325°F/Gas 3 and cook for a further hour or until a skewer inserted into the centre of the cake comes out clean. Cover the top with greaseproof paper during cooking to prevent over-browning.
5. Invert the cake on to a wire rack and leave to cool.

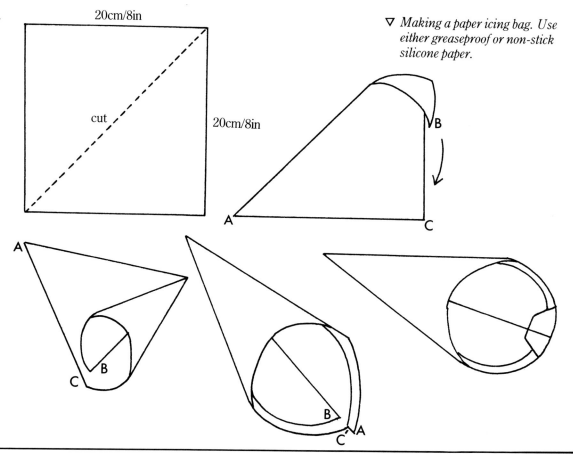

▽ *Making a paper icing bag. Use either greaseproof or non-stick silicone paper.*

53

Ingredients

50g/2oz/good ¼ cup soft
    brown sugar
50g/2oz/¼ cup butter or solid
    margarine
5 level tablespoons clear
    honey
½ tsp ground ginger
½ tsp mixed spice
½ tsp ground cinnamon
200g/8oz/2 cups plain
    (all-purpose) flour
½ tsp bicarbonate of soda
White marzipan or sugarpaste
    for decorating if desired

Makes 4 'adults' and 6 'children'.

Method

1. Place sugar and butter or margarine in a saucepan over a low heat. Carefully measure in the honey and heat the mixture gently until the fat has melted. Remove the pan from the heat.
2. Sift the spices and flour on to a plate.
3. Mix the bicarbonate of soda and water together and add to the pan with the flour, stirring well until the mixture leaves the side of the pan and begins to form a ball.
4. Allow to cool slightly, then turn the dough on to a lightly floured surface and knead until smooth, then wrap and leave until cold.
5. Preheat the oven to 190°C/375°F/Gas 5. Brush a large baking sheet with oil. Make the bear templates using card.
6. Roll out the dough 0.5cm/¼in thick and cut carefully round the templates. Lift the bears on to the baking sheet, leaving a little space between each one. Mark round the edges of the ears and paws to define them with a small pointed knife.
7. Bake in the centre of the oven for 10 to 12 minutes until lightly browned. Lift off and leave to cool on a wire rack. The biscuits will quickly harden, but will soften slightly in texture after a few hours which is characteristic of this kind of biscuit.

To Dress the Bears

1. The bears can be 'dressed' in any way you like. Use either white marzipan or sugarpaste (see page 49) for the clothes, and colour small quantities of it with paste food colourings or paint on the colour after the biscuits have been dressed.
2. Use the biscuit templates as a guide to size, adding on a little extra at the sides to account for the spreading and depth of the cooked biscuits.
3. Stick the clothes on to the biscuits with a little honey.
4. Finish the biscuits by painting patches and designs on the clothes, and features and paws on the bears.

Measure the honey accurately with a warm spoon. Level the spoon with a knife and scrape off excess underneath.

DAD   BABY   MUM

Bear family biscuits.

Chocolate Teddies

These make delightful sweets or little presents, as well as being a surprise filling for the cake.

Ingredients

250g/8oz white or dessert chocolate
Powder food colourings (for white chocolate only)
Several small greaseproof paper piping bags (see page 52).

Method

1. Trace or draw the teddy outlines shown on page 60 on to a thin piece of white card, leaving a small space between each one. Stick the card on to a flat portable surface such as a chopping board. Pin a smooth piece of waxed or non-stick baking parchment over the card.
2. Break up the chocolate and place it in a small bowl over a pan of hot water until it has melted. Alternatively, heat in the microwave on Medium for 2 to 3 minutes or until soft when pierced with a fork. Do not overheat.
3. Stir a little coloured powder into the chocolate until it is evenly tinted, if desired.

4. Place a little melted chocolate in the piping bag and snip off the tip. Pipe the chocolate round the outline of four or five shapes, omitting the ears. Return to the first shape and press out the chocolate, moving the bag backwards and forwards inside the shape to fill as thickly as possible, using a new bag when necessary.
5. Finely pipe the ears, making sure they touch the head where appropriate, and pipe extra chocolate for the snout.
6. Leave the shapes to set before piping a contrasting colour on top, if desired.
7. When dry, carefully cut the paper round each one and leave attached. Store flat in a cool place.

If the chocolate sets in the piping bag it can be placed in the microwave for a few seconds to soften. Alternatively, it can be mixed with a little melted butter or a teaspoonful of icing sugar.

If using several colours, divide the chocolate into small containers such as egg cups and stand these in a roasting tin containing a little hot water. Do not allow water or steam to reach the chocolate.

Marzipan Bears

Ingredients

200g/8oz white marzipan
Brown paste food colouring

Makes 4 bears.

Method

Note: the bears may be made brown with white features or white with brown features.
1. Knead a little colouring into half the marzipan.
2. Reserve a pea-sized piece of white marzipan and a similar piece of brown for the features.
3. Cut each large piece of marzipan in half and keep the pieces wrapped until ready to use.

▽ *Making marzipan bears.*

To Mould the Bears

1. Take one portion of marzipan and cut off a small piece for the arms. Mould and cut the remaining piece to make the body (step 1).
2. Sit the bear up and smooth the legs, pulling up a piece at the ends to make the feet (steps 2 and 3).
3. Cut the arm pieces as shown and smooth them on to the sides of the body. Press out the ends to make the paws.
4. Mould the face and snout and pull out the sides of the head to form the ears (step 3).
5. Using the contrasting colour, press tiny pieces of marzipan on the ears, paws and feet. Roll tiny balls for the eyes and nose, and press into position (step 4).

The bears make ideal table decorations or, wrapped up, charming party presents for children. They can also be used to decorate cakes.

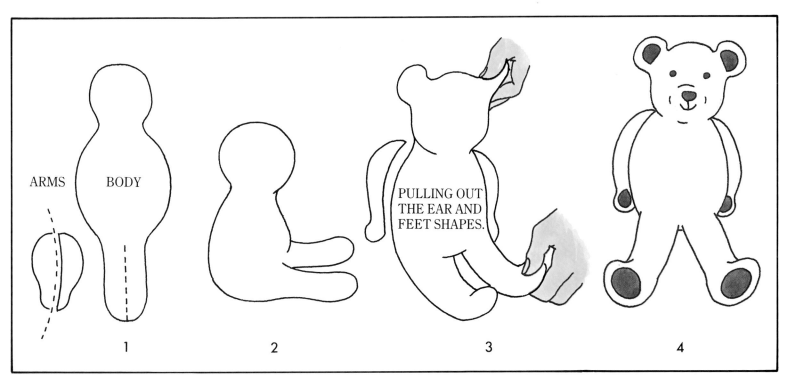

ARMS   BODY

PULLING OUT THE EAR AND FEET SHAPES.

1   2   3   4

Preparation for piping or run-outs.

Paper with teddy patterns.

Waxed or non-stick paper pinned over patterns.

board

A = teddy for small biscuits 64mm/2½in long.   B = teddy for large biscuits 76mm/3in long, and for smaller chocolate bears to fit inside cake.   C = large teddy for chocolate sweets.

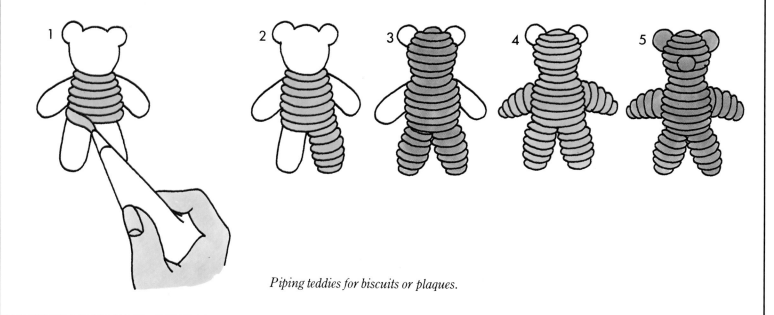

Piping teddies for biscuits or plaques.

These biscuits are ideal for christenings or young children's parties.

Ingredients

100g/4oz/1 cup
    plain/(all-purpose) flour
50g/2oz/¼ cup butter,
    softened
50g/2oz/⅓ cup castor
    (superfine) sugar
2 egg yolks
2 tsp finely grated lemon rind
Makes 8 large and 8 small
    biscuits (using 7.5cm/3in
    and 6cm/2½in oval cutters)

Royal Icing
1 egg white
200g/8oz/2 cups icing
    (confectioners') sugar,
    sifted
Pink or blue food colouring

Method

1. Preheat the oven to 190°C/375°F/Gas 5. Grease a baking sheet.
2. Sift the flour into a bowl, make a well in the centre and add the butter, sugar, egg yolks and lemon rind.
3. Using either the fingers or a large fork, work the flour into the ingredients to form a soft dough.
4. Knead the dough lightly on a floured surface until smooth then roll it out thickly and cut out the biscuits.
5. Place the smaller biscuits in the centre of the prepared baking sheet and cut a hole in each using the end of a plastic straw. Arrange the larger biscuits around them and bake for ten to twelve minutes until lightly browned. Lift the biscuits on to a wire rack to cool.

To Decorate the Biscuits

Royal Icing

1. Place the egg white in a clean grease-free bowl and stir in two-thirds of the icing sugar.
2. Beat the icing hard with a clean wooden spoon until thick and fluffy, gradually adding the remaining icing sugar until the icing is stiff and forms soft peaks. It should be stiff enough to hold its shape when piped but soft enough to pipe into a line. Cover the icing until ready to use.

Teddy Bears

These can be piped either directly on to the biscuits or on to waxed or non-stick paper and then stuck on the biscuits when dry. Prepare the paper as for Chocolate Teddies (page 57).

1. Tint the icing as required and place a small quantity in a greaseproof paper piping bag (see page 52). Snip off the tip and put the nozzle into position.
2. Squeeze out the icing and rotate the nozzle to form a thick coil the width of the teddy's body. Keep rotating the nozzle, making the coils close together as you make your way slowly down the body and the legs. Pipe several bodies at the same time (steps 1 and 2 of diagram on page 60).
3. Pipe the heads omitting the ears, then the arms (steps 3 and 4).
4. After a few minutes to let the icing dry pipe on the snout and ears (step 5).
5. When quite dry paint on the eyes and nose if desired.

To Finish the Biscuits

1. Using a fine nozzle, pipe a row of small dots round the edge of the larger biscuits.
2. Dust them with castor sugar.
3. Tie a narrow piece of ribbon through the holes in the smaller biscuits.

Bears to Bake

Materials

225g/8oz/2 cups plain (all-purpose) flour
100g/4oz/5 tablespoons salt
100ml/4 fluid oz/½ cup cold water

Method

1. Mix the flour with the salt, which acts as a preservative, then work in about 100ml/4 fluid oz cold water to make a soft dough.
2. Knead the dough lightly until it is smooth and malleable. In this form it may be stored in a polythene bag in the refrigerator. It may also be coloured with non-toxic colours.
3. Roll out the dough, shape it into bears, or whatever shape you wish, and bake it at 140°C/275°F/Gas mark 1, until it is crisp and dry. Depending on the thickness and size of the shapes you make this takes between one and two hours. Drying the dough in stages in residual oven heat also works.
4. When the shapes are dry, paint and varnish them. They can be used to make models for children to play with, wall plaques, buttons, jewellery, party presents or simply delightful ornaments.
5. If the oven is too hot the dough will darken and be unsuitable for painting. Adding a little cooking oil will make the dough less brittle for delicate items such as thin buttons or earrings.

BEARS
TO SEW

Motifs for traycloth.

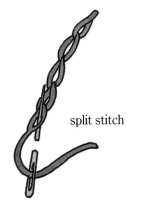

split stitch

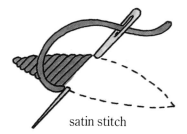

satin stitch

Design

The design shown in the book was drawn freehand, the idea being not to make the traycloth look too formal. Try to make your own design, but if you wish to copy this one, trace it on a piece of tracing or greaseproof paper with a soft pencil. Lay the pencil side down on the material and go over the wrong side of the paper with a pencil. The outline will come out faintly on the cloth, and can be made sharper with a sharp pencil. The circles were made with a cake plate (to give a fluted edge), one traced slightly off centre and the other placed on top and drawn 1cm/½in under the line at the top and 1cm/½in below the line at the bottom. It gives a more attractive look than a perfect circle drawn exactly in the centre. The honey pots do not match exactly at the corners, again to give a casual look. The bees are a little more exact in position.

The stitch used is split stitch throughout (as shown in diagram), this gives a neat line. The body of the bees, the bows, the soles of the bears' feet and paws, the spoons and the tops of the honeypots are worked in satin stitch (as shown in diagram) to give a depth of colour.

The word 'honey' on the pots is done in straight stitch with one thread or black cotton if you prefer.

Make a 1cm/½in hem round the cloth and hem if possible, it shows less than machining. Sew on the lace trimming, straight pleating it to go round the corners. Use Sylko thread to match the linen and lace.

Honey Pot Cover

Most attractive teddy bear design fabric can be bought from shops that sell patchwork material, and this makes dainty covers for marmalade or honey pots.

Materials

0.25 metre/¼ yd figured cotton
0.75 metre/¾ yd narrow lace trimming
0.25 metre/¼ yd narrow elastic
Matching sewing thread

Method 1

1. Cut a 23cm/9in diameter circle in the cotton fabric. Draw an inner circle on the material with a 16cm/6in diameter.
2. Cut on the bias a strip 4 cm/1½in wide and about 45cm/18in long.
3. Turn and sew a narrow hem round the outer edge of the circle, and trim it with gathered narrow lace.
4. Turn in the edges of the bias strip and sew it round the inner drawn circle on the right side, leaving an opening for inserting the elastic. Thread narrow elastic through, and fasten off. Neaten the bias strip where open. Your cover is now ready to pop over the pot.

Teddy Motifs

△
Some ideas for sew-on teddy motifs.

Method 2

1. For this method you also need 0.25 metre/¼ yd plain fabric. Cut out two circles of material with a diameter of 23cms/9in, one patterned and the other plain in a contrasting colour.
2. With right sides together stitch round the outside edge leaving a small opening for turning right side out.
3. Turn right side out, stitch up the opening and press.
4. Draw an inner circle on the lining material with a diameter of 16cm/6in. Draw another circle within it leaving sufficient room between the two to thread through the elastic.
5. Stitch round both circles.
6. Trim the outside edge with lace.
7. Make a small cut to insert the elastic, thread it through and fasten it off.

These motifs can be sewn on to jumpers, tee-shirts, bags, jeans, and so on. They are best made in strong, plain cotton material. If your material is a little thin, stick iron-on interfacing on the back before embroidering.

Materials

Cotton fabric
Tracing paper
Sharp scissors
Embroidery thread
Interfacing (optional)

Method

1. Draw or trace your favourite teddy bear shape on to tracing or greaseproof paper with an HB pencil.
2. Turn the paper over and place on the right side of the material and then trace over the lines, thereby transferring the design. If you prefer, you can use a transfer needlework pencil and iron the shape on to the material like a transfer.
3. Buttonhole stitch round the outline of the drawing and use back stitch on the inner lines.
4. Embroider in the features and then using sharp pointed scissors cut carefully round the edge of your motif. It is now ready to be sewn on.

Jacket

Method

Instructions are given for a suit to fit a two- to four-year-old, though the pattern could be adapted for larger sizes. The suit is reversible.

Materials

1 metre/1 yard of 115cm/45in of main fabric, lining and wadding
Pieces of bright fabric for motifs
Iron-on interfacing
3.5 metres/3½ yards bias binding to tone or contrast
6 toggles
Matching thread

1. From the main fabric, lining and wadding, cut out one jacket back, two fronts (reverse one to get a left and a right side) and one collar piece. Cut the wadding slightly larger than the pattern for ease of making up.
2. Iron the fabric for appliqué on to the interfacing, and draw the motifs on the interfaced side. Cut out, and using a pencil, lightly draw in the features on the right side.
3. **Appliqué motifs.** Lay the top fabric (right side uppermost) on the wadding and pin it in place. Using a zig-zag stitch, sew neatly round the edges to secure the wadding. Trim off the excess wadding.
4. Arrange the motifs on the jacket pieces, allowing approximately 11cm/4in for the overlap and toggles on one front, and secure them with pins.
5. Set your sewing-machine on a medium to wide satin stitch. Using a buttonhole foot if possible, zig-zag round the motifs in the order shown in the diagrams. You can use either a matching or contrasting thread for this.
6. Using a narrower satin stitch, sew the teddy bears' features. This could also be done by hand. Pull all the threads through to the back, and fasten off by hand.

7. **Assembling the jacket.** With right sides together, pin, baste and stitch the shoulder seams and underarm seams. Reinforce the underarms with an extra row of stitches. Clip the curve, and neaten the seams.
8. Pin the top collar fabric to the wadding and zig-zag in place. Trim the wadding.
9. With right sides together and the raw edges aligned, stitch the collar on to the neck edge of the jacket.
10. Repeat steps 7 to 9 with the lining, omitting the wadding.
11. Slip the lining into the jacket with wrong sides together.
12. **Binding.** Take a piece of bias binding at least 24cm/9in long and fold its edges towards the middle. Machine stitch, making a long narrow strip.
13. Cut the strip into three 8cm/3in lengths.
14. Turn the jacket to the wrong side. Pin and tack the lining to the padded jacket all round the edges and sleeves, matching the corners and seams.
15. Fold the narrow binding strips in half to make loops and pin at regular intervals down the front on the inside, starting approximately 2.5cm/1in from the collar seam, so that the raw edges will be caught when the binding is stitched in place.

16. Take the rest of the binding, open out one folded edge and pin to the wrong side of the jacket with the raw edges matching. Machine stitch the binding along the fold line, around the fronts, collar, back and ends of the sleeves.
17. Turn the jacket to the right side and fold the binding over to cover the stitch line. Machine stitch the binding in place.
18. **Finishing the toggle loops.** Fold the loops towards the front and machine in place, making several rows of stitching on the binding.
19. Attach the toggles on the opposite front to correspond with the loops. If the jacket is to be made reversible, toggles must be attached to both sides of this front.

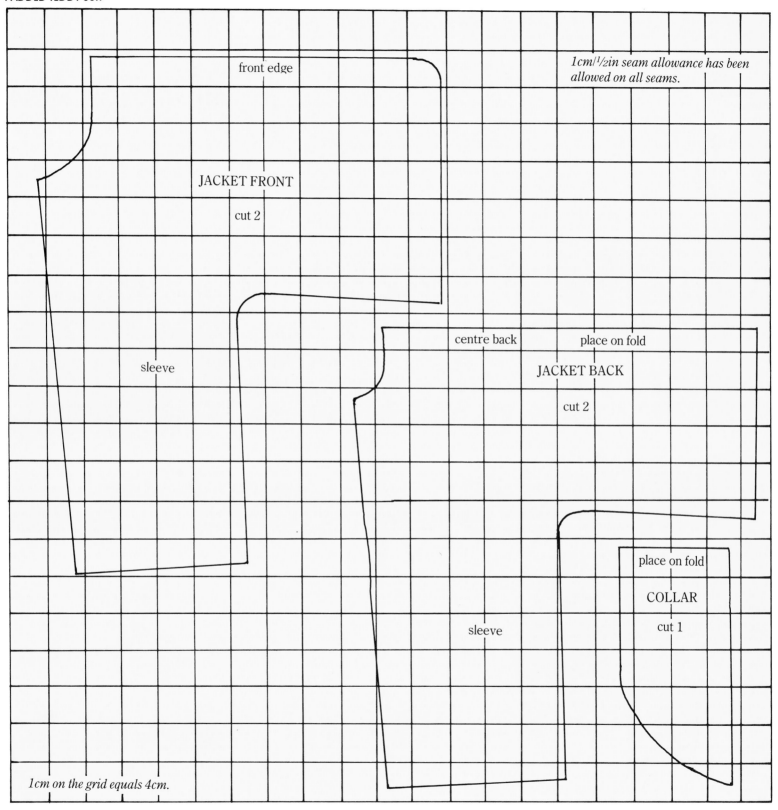

front edge

1cm/½in seam allowance has been allowed on all seams.

JACKET FRONT

cut 2

sleeve

centre back

place on fold

JACKET BACK

cut 2

sleeve

place on fold

COLLAR

cut 1

1cm on the grid equals 4cm.

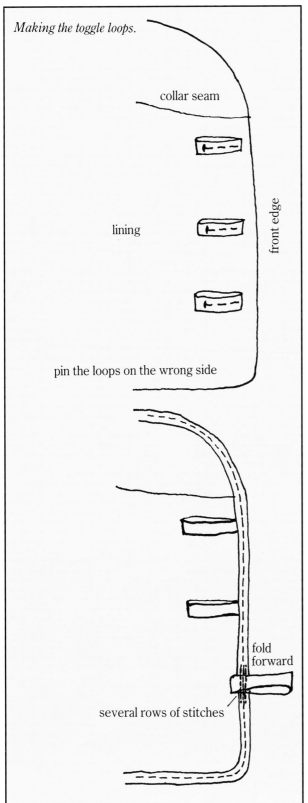

Making the toggle loops.

collar seam

lining

front edge

pin the loops on the wrong side

fold forward

several rows of stitches

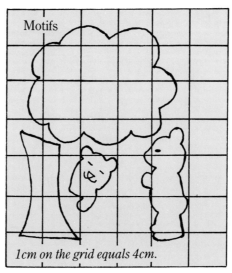

Motifs

1cm on the grid equals 4cm.

cut 2

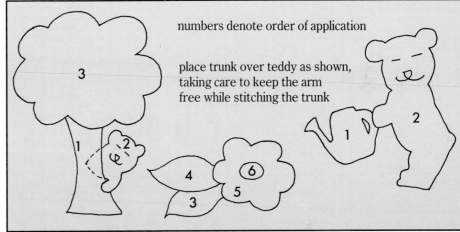

numbers denote order of application

place trunk over teddy as shown,
taking care to keep the arm
free while stitching the trunk

3

1

2

4

3

5

6

1

2

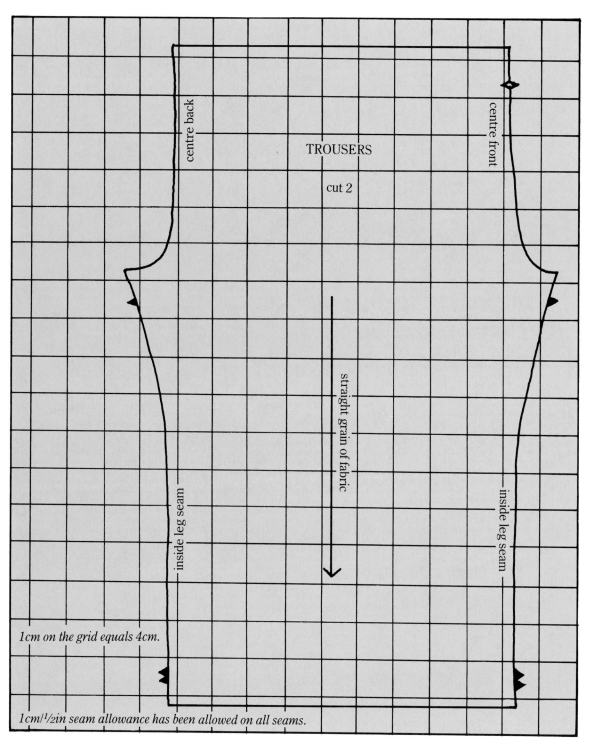

centre back

TROUSERS

cut 2

centre front

straight grain of fabric

inside leg seam

inside leg seam

1cm on the grid equals 4cm.

1cm/½in seam allowance has been allowed on all seams.

Trousers

Materials

80cm/31in of 115cm/45in of main fabric, lining and wadding
80cm/31in bias binding
2.5cm/1in wide elastic to fit waist

Method

1. Cut out two pieces from top fabric, lining and wadding, remembering to cut the wadding generously. Make sure you cut out a right leg and a left leg by reversing the pattern.
2. Lay the top fabric right side uppermost on the wadding and pin it in place. Zig-zag neatly round the edge to secure the wadding, and trim off the excess wadding.
3. Take one trouser leg, fold it with right sides together, matching the points, and stitch the inside leg seam.
4. Repeat with the other leg.
5. Turn one leg right side out and slip it into the other leg, so the right sides are together. Match the stitch the crutch seam, and reinforce it with a second line of stitching. Trim the seam and clip the curve. Pull the inside leg back out again. The trousers are now wrong side out.
6. Repeat step 5 with the lining, omitting the wadding.

7. Turn the lining right side out and slip it inside the trousers, so the right sides of the lining and trousers are together. Pin the waist edges together, then stitch 1cm/½in from the raw edge, leaving a gap of 4cm/1½in for inserting the elastic.

8. Turn the trousers through *one* leg to the right side, and pull the lining into position. Top stitch round the waist edge, again leaving the gap for the elastic.

9. Make the casing for the elastic by machining 4cm/1½in below the top stitching all around the trouser waist.

10. Thread the elastic through and stitch the ends. Neaten the gap with top stitching.

11. To keep the elastic in place, top stitch over the elastic in two rows, pulling the elastic taut either side of the presser foot as you stitch. This gives a professional looking finish.

12. To finish, bind the bottom of the trouser legs as you did the edges of the jacket.

Teddy Bear Sampler

74

Materials

33cm/13in × 28cm/11in 14
    count Fine Aida
    needlework fabric
One skein each of the
    following DMC stranded
    cotton:
    973 yellow
    972 orange
    310 black
    797 blue
    612 light brown
    370 brown
    610 dark brown
    3031 very dark brown
    3033 fawn
Embroidery frame
    approximately 20cm/8in
    (not essential)
2-4 embroidery needles

Method

1. Fasten the material into a
frame and pull it taut.
2. Start the work from the middle
of the pattern to ensure that the
finished sampler is correctly sited.
The middle is clearly marked on all
sides of the grid.
3. Use two strands of thread and
work from the middle in even
cross stitch. As the sampler
grows so more needles can come
into use, each threaded with a
different colour cotton. When not
in use the spare needles can be
carefully stored at the edge of the
work.
4. All outlining should be done in
back stitch. Outlining for the
central teddy bear should be
worked in 3031 very dark brown.
5. Next work the 'Teddy Bear'
lettering in cross stitch. This is
not outlined.
6. Finally work the border. Note
that all the flowers are fully
outlined in 610 dark brown.
7. The bees' wings are worked in
back stitch only, in 310 black.
8. Finally press your finished
work on the back only. This helps
to 'lift' the stitching on the right
side.
9. If wanted the finished sampler
can be mounted on hard card.

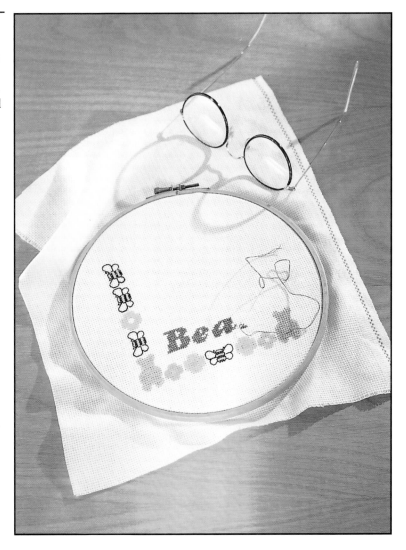

Stitch by stitch grid for the sampler.
The arrows indicate the centres of
each side.

Moneybags Bear

Materials

42cm/16in × 30cm/12in fur
    fabric with pile running
    downwards on the
    30cm/12in side
Small piece of felt or suede for
    soles of feet
46cm/18in of 2cm/¾in wide
    ribbon for bow round neck
Small piece of matching
    material for lining
9cm/3½in long zip fastener
40cm/15½in matching braid
    5cm/2in wide for handle
Matching sewing thread
Pair 1cm/½in diameter safety
    eyes
Black embroidery cotton for
    nose and mouth
Handful of polyester for
    stuffing

Method

1. Cut one back and two fronts in fur fabric, the second in reverse. Cut on the wrong side with the tips of the scissors to prevent cutting the pile.
2. Using stab stitch (see page 10) and with right sides of the fur fabric facing, stitch from A - C on the front pieces.
3. Fasten in the eyes and stitch the nose and mouth with black embroidery cotton.
4. Cut the back piece from E - F and sew the zip fastener into this opening with the zip opening from top to bottom.
5. Put the back and fronts together with right sides facing, and stitch from A - B on both sides of the head.
6. Stitch from B to D on both sides.
7. Cut two soles in leather or suede and sew into the foot, matching D - G. Repeat on the other side.
8. Stitch the legs from C - G on the front, which will be F - G on the back.

9. Turn right side out. If the pile is thick this will take a little time. Use a pencil or strong stick to push the arms out.
10. Stuff lightly the head, arms, legs and feet.
11. Mark the neck, tops of the arms and tops of the legs with stab stitch, where shown with a dotted line. This will keep the stuffing in place and leave room in the body for the purse.
12. Cut two pieces of lining and sew round the curved edge. This fits into the stomach of the bear.

13. Place the lining in position, making sure that the wrong side faces the inside of the bear. Turn the rough edges under and sew to the zip fastener braid round the opening.
14. Tie a bow round the neck of the bear.
15. Fold the matching braid in half. Turn the rough edges under and oversew to neaten. Sew on to the bear through the ribbon at the back of the neck. To finish off, make a few stitches at the join of the legs to turn the feet forwards.

A
+

B

FRONT

cut 2,
1 in reverse

C

D   G

↓ direction of pile

*Pattern for Moneybags Bear.
1cm on the grid equals 2cm.*

BACK
cut 1

E

← opening

F

D   G   G   D

sew this side
to zip opening

LINING

cut 2

D   SOLE
    cut 2   G

Method

The bees are fastened on by press-studs so they can easily be removed for washing.

Materials

1 metre/1 yard cotton fabric
3 metres/3 yards matching
  narrow cord
Approximately 225g/8oz
  polyester stuffing
Oddments of white and brown
  felt
Matching thread
Yellow embroidery thread

BEE

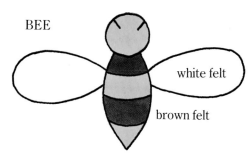

white felt

brown felt

1. To make the cosy fit your teapot exactly, take the following measurements.
Strip 1: measure round the widest part of the teapot and add a quarter.
E.g. width = 48cm/19in + 12cm/5in = 60cm/24in.
Strip 2: halve the above length and deduct 2cm/¾in.
E.g. 30cm/12in − 2cm/¾in = 28cm/11¼in.
Strip 3: take length of Strip 2 and deduct 2cm/¾in.
E.g. 28cm/11¼in − 2cm/¾in = 26cm/10½in.
Strip 4: deduct 4cm/1½in from double the length of Strip 3.
E.g. 52cm/20in − 4cm/1½in = 48cm/18½in.
2. Cut from cotton fabric:
One piece of Strip 1 12cm/4½in wide.
Two pieces of Strip 2 12cm/4½in wide.
Two pieces of Strip 3 12cm/4½in wide.
One piece of Strip 4 12cm/4½in wide.
3. Strip 1. Join the short edges. Fold in half and sew 1mm from the edge all round, leaving an opening of 10cm/4in. Fill lightly with polyester and sew up the opening.
4. Strip 2. Sew the short edge of each strip. Fold in half and sew 1mm from the edge along the length. Fill each piece with polyester and sew up.

5. Strip 3. Sew the short edge of each strip. Fold in half and sew 1mm from the edge along the length. Fill each piece with polyester and sew up.
6. Strip 4. Join the short edges. Fold in half and sew 1mm from the edge all round, leaving an opening of 10cm/4in. Fill lightly with polyester and sew up the opening.
7. Sew Strip 1 to Strip 2; Strip 3 to Strip 2; Strip 4 to Strip 3. There will be openings for the handle and spout between strips 2 and 3. Gather the top of Strip 4, pull up tightly and fasten off. The tea-cosy is now ready for finishing.
8. Cover the seams on the outside with matching cord, including the openings for the spout and handle. When fastening the cord on the wrong side of the tea-cosy, tie a knot to prevent the cord from unravelling.
9. To make the bees, cut out wings in white felt, and two bodies in brown felt. Sew the body pieces together, stuff lightly, and sew up. Stripe the body by stitching round it with yellow embroidery thread. Sew on the wings.
10. Sew a press-stud on the underside of each bee, and its other half where you want to position the bees on the tea-cosy.

Pyjama Case

Method

Case

1. Cut the cotton, wadding and lining to measure 46cm/18in wide × 66cm/26in long and place them on top of each other, right side down.
2. Pin the layers together, tack and then sew or machine round two long sides and one short side. (Do not skip the pinning and tacking or the material will move and be spoilt when machining or sewing.)
3. Turn right side out and press lightly. Inevitably a little wadding will have moved, trim this off.
4. Turn in the raw edge and oversew with matching thread. Fold 23cm/9in up and 8cm/3in down and stitch the zip fastener into position. This is the back of the case and the fastener runs the length of it. If your fastener is 30cm/12in long there will be approximately 5cm/2in of opening left each side of it. Close these by oversewing.
5. Sew on the trimming round the outer edge.

Pillow

1. Cut material 18cm/7in × 24cm/9in and fold in half giving a shape 18cm/7in × 12cm/4½in. Sew together on the long and one short side.
2. Turn right side out, press, and lightly fill with polyester.
3. Oversew the open side.
4. Trim round the outer edge with gathered lace.

Cover

1. Cut material 52cm/20in long × 18cm/7in wide and fold in half to make a piece measuring 26cm/10in × 18cm/7in.
2. Cut a strip 6cm/2in wide and 148cm/58in long. Fold in half widthwise and press.
3. Pleat this strip by leaving 2cm/¾in and pleating 2cm/¾in under (making 2cm/¾in of trimming from 4cm/1½in of material). Continue along the length of the strip and machine or sew to keep in place.
4. Place the material right side up and pin the trimming on top of it round one short and two long sides with the folded edge facing in and the rough edge facing out. Place the other piece of material on top, right side down, sandwiching the trimming. Pin, tack and stitch all round the two long sides and the short side. Turn right side out and press lightly.
5. Place a handful of stuffing inside, pushing it down to leave approximately 4cm at the top unstuffed to turn over. Turn in and oversew the open side and trim with 1cm/½in wide gathered lace.

Materials

Case

44cm/17in wide × 66cm/26in long cotton fabric
44cm/17in × 66cm/26in matching lining fabric
Matching sewing thread
40cm/16in or 30cm/12in zip fastener
44cm/17in × 66cm/26in medium thickness wadding
Approximately 2 metres/2 yards 1.5cm/¾in wide trimming

Pillow

18cm × 24cm/7in × 9in white cotton material
Approximately 2 metres/2 yards 1cm/½in wide white lace
White sewing thread
Handful polyester stuffing

Cover

52cm/20in long × 18cm/7in wide thin cotton material
A strip of the same material 6cm/2in wide × approximately 148cm/58in long
Handful polyester stuffing
Matching sewing thread

Bear*

36cm/14in × 40cm/16in fur fabric (pile to run downwards on the 36cm/14in width)
Black embroidery cotton for eyes, mouth and nose.
Approximately 42cm/16in narrow ribbon for neck
Matching sewing thread

* Your own favourite bear could be used instead.

Bear

1. Cut two pieces of the bear pattern in fur fabric with the pile running down.

2. Embroider the eyes, nose and mouth on the front piece with black cotton.

3. Place the two pieces together with right sides facing and pin, tack and stitch round the outer edge leaving an opening for turning. (Do not omit to pin and tack or the fur fabric will move when sewing and spoil the shape of the bear.)

4. Turn right side out, stuff lightly and oversew the open seam.

5. Tie the ribbon round the bear's neck.

6. Mark where shown with dots the ears, neck, tops of the arms and tops of the legs by slip-stitching.

7. Slip-stitch the pillow and cover on to the top side of the pyjama case, remembering to turn back about 4cm of the cover. Place the bear in the bed and your pyjama case is ready for use.

Pyjama case bear. ▷

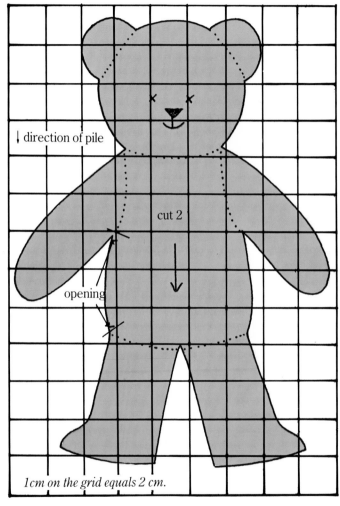

↓ direction of pile

cut 2

opening

1cm on the grid equals 2 cm.

BEARS
IN CARD,
PAPER
AND
WOOD

Child's Brooch   Card Toys   Bear Up a Stick

86

This little brooch has a movable head, arms and legs. It can be made with any expression you like, and decorated in any way.

The brooch pieces. The dots mark ▷ where the holes should be made.

Materials

Tracing paper
Thin card
Mounting board
Craft knife
Split pins (2 per brooch)
Safety pin
Felt pens, crayons or paints
Darning needle
Fine knitting needle
Plastic repair tape

Method

1. Trace the pattern on to tracing paper and transfer it to thin card to act as your template. Cut out all the pieces in thin card.
2. Trace round the card templates to mark out the bear on to thick mounting board. The patterns can be turned round to make the bear face the other way.
3. Cut the shapes out of the mounting board with a craft knife.

4. Using felt pens, crayons or paints, draw in the bear's eyes, nose, mouth and claws in black. Paint or draw on the clothes, using whatever patterns you like. Then colour in the bear's fur – this is best done with paint.
5. Make holes in the lower part of the neck, the top and bottom of the body, and the tops of the arms and legs. Start by using a large darning needle and then enlarge the holes with a fine knitting needle. Do not make the holes too big. The joints need to be a little stiff so the bear will stay in whatever position you put him.
6. Sandwich the body and neck between the arms and push a split pin through the holes to hold it all together. Then put each leg on opposite sides of the body and push the other split pin through the holes to hold them in place.
7. Attach a safety pin to the back of the head with plastic repair tape, sticking the tape to the back of the pin. The brooch is now ready to wear.

Card Toys

If the bears are made in thin card children can cut them out themselves and make a whole family of bears to play with. Girl bears can be given a skirt from the pattern shown. Bend the skirt forward a little to keep it clear of the leg movement. By changing the shape of the mouth and eyes, the bears can be made to look happy, sad or angry.

Bear Up a Stick

Simple stick puppets can be made by attaching a bear made to the brooch pattern above to a short cane (we used green garden canes). The bear is glued to the cane, and the join is reinforced with plastic repair tape.

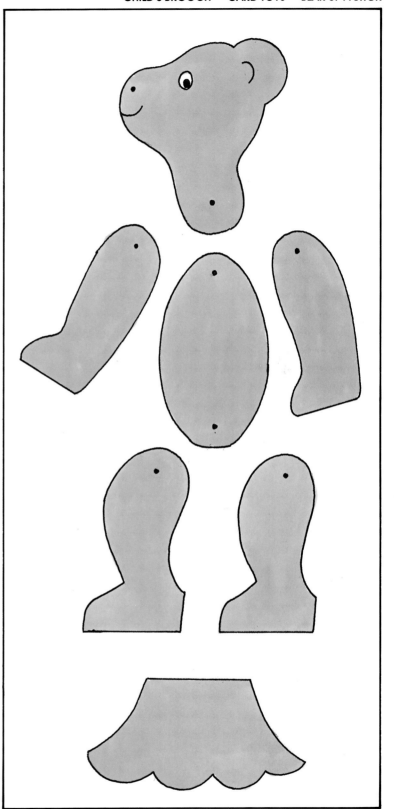

Lino Cuts

Here are two simple printing techniques that will enable you to create a wide variety of bears in action. The designs can be used to make a frieze for a child's bedroom, to decorate a bedside lamp, a bag, or table mats, to personalize stationery, and so on. Water-based printing inks are the easiest to use, but if you want to print on a fabric which will need washing, e.g. a child's T-shirt, then you should use a suitable fabric ink. Check in a craft shop that you are buying the right ink for the right purpose.

Materials

Small pieces of lino
Lino-cutting knife
Small block(s) of wood
Glue
Biscuit tin lid
Water-based paper inks or
   fabric inks
Small roller

Printing on paper or card.
▽

Method

1. You can create your own design or trace those shown here. If the latter, trace the design and transfer it to the lino. Cut away the shaded area with a lino tool, and stick the lino on to a small block of wood, which forms a handle.
2. A biscuit tin lid or other flat surface makes a good ink tray. Squeeze 2cm/¾in or so from a tube of water-based printing ink in your chosen colour and spread it evenly on the lid with the roller.
3. Run the roller over the ink and then use it to coat the lino evenly.

4. Press the lino firmly on your chosen surface to make a print. If printing on paper you may need to rub the reverse side of the paper with the back of a spoon to press it on to the lino block and ensure a full, clear print. If doing largish prints on fabric you may need a soft base on which to lay the material for printing. You can make one by covering a board with a thin layer of foam plastic, and stretching a polythene sheet over the top, fixed to the underneath of the board with sticky tape.

Teddy drawn on lino ready to be carved out with a lino tool.

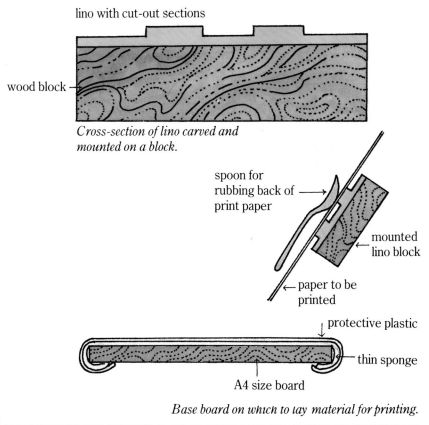

lino with cut-out sections

wood block →

Cross-section of lino carved and mounted on a block.

spoon for rubbing back of print paper →

mounted lino block ←

← paper to be printed

protective plastic ↓

thin sponge →

A4 size board

Base board on which to lay material for printing.

◁ shapes for the kite

◁ shapes for the scooter and juggler
(see page 93)

Shapes suitable for printing.

A permanent marker can be used to draw the string.

The scooter is made from three repeated shapes. Print the teddy first, then add the scooter base, then the upright, and lastly the handlebar and wheels.

Carrot Prints

Method

1. The fat carrot cut diagonally (Cut 1) makes an oval shape for teddy's body; cut straight across (Cut 2) it makes a round shape for its head. The thin carrot cut diagonally (Cut 3) makes the arm and leg shapes; cut straight across (Cut 4) it makes the ear shape. Cut the carrots to give the shapes you want.

2. The biscuit tin lid is used as an ink tray. Squeeze 2cm or so from the ink tube into the lid and use the small roller to spread it evenly.

3. Start with the fat oblong shape, Cut 1. Dip it into the ink, make sure it is well coated, and press it firmly on to the paper to make the teddy's body.

4. Repeat with the fat circle, Cut 2, to make the head.

5. Repeat with the thin oblongs, Cut 3, to make the arms and legs. These can be positioned as you like to make the teddy stand, run, sit or play.

6. Finally add the small circles, Cut 4, to make the ears.

7. Straight cuts from further along the thin carrot can be printed in other colours to make balls for juggling, and so on.

▷

Materials

A fat carrot
A thin carrot
Sharp knife
Water-based paper inks or
    fabric inks
Biscuit tin lid
Small roller

A teddy created from the cuts shown above. On the finished teddy the overlap of shapes will not be seen.

Carrot printing.

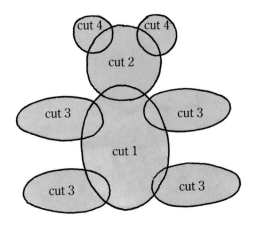

Teddy Bookmark

A juggling teddy is an excellent subject for a bookmark.

Materials

Thin card in a light colour
Pair of compasses
Ruler
Scissors
Letraset (optional)

Method

1. From the card cut a rectangle measuring 222mm × 76mm/ 8¼in × 3in.
2. Using a pair of compasses, draw a semi-circle at the top and cut round it carefully.
3. Choose the bear motif you want (see pages 90 and 91) and print it just higher than the centre of the bookmark. If you use the juggling teddy, space the balls to follow the curve at the top of the bookmark. Leave the print to dry.
4. Draw 12mm/½in spaces for each line of lettering, allowing 6mm/¼in spaces between. Leave 12mm/½in space at the bottom of the card.
5. Lightly mark the centre of each line, and divide the letters so that you have equal numbers on each side of the centre line. Outline the letters in soft pencil, and then complete them with inks, paints or crayons, or use Letraset for a professional look.
6. Lightly remove the guidelines you have drawn with a soft eraser when the lettering is completed.

◁
A design suitable for a bookmark.

93

Sky-diving Bears Mobile

Method

This brightly coloured mobile is easy to make and will delight a small child.

Materials

1 23cm/9in craft canes
2 15cm/6in craft canes
Coloured paper
Card
Thread
Double-sided adhesive tape
Glue
Scissors

1. To make each parachute canopy you need an A5/5¾in × 8¼in sheet of coloured paper. Bright colours are best for a small child's room. Draw a line 76mm/3in from one short side. This forms section A in the diagram.
2. Divide the remainder, marked B in the diagram, into 6mm/½in strips from the line to the other end of the paper. Don't worry about the small strip left over.

3. Fold over a 6mm/½in strip, C, at the edge of portion B. Cut through both C and B along the lines you have drawn.
4. Turn the paper over, and stick a strip of double-sided adhesive tape to the top edge of A. Then stick a strip along one side of A, as shown in the diagram. You are now ready to form the canopy.
5. Stick the two short sides of A together to form a tube, with the double-sided tape at the long end of A inside the tube.

6. Starting with the strip nearest the join in the tube, bend the strips, B, outwards, and tuck portion C of each strip inside the tube to adhere to the double-sided tape at its edge. Side by side, these strips fit the circumference of the tube exactly. The narrower strip which is left over should be cut off. You will now have a parachute canopy.
7. Trace the teddies on to the card and cut them out. There are four per mobile.

Shapes for the bears and parachute harness for the mobile.

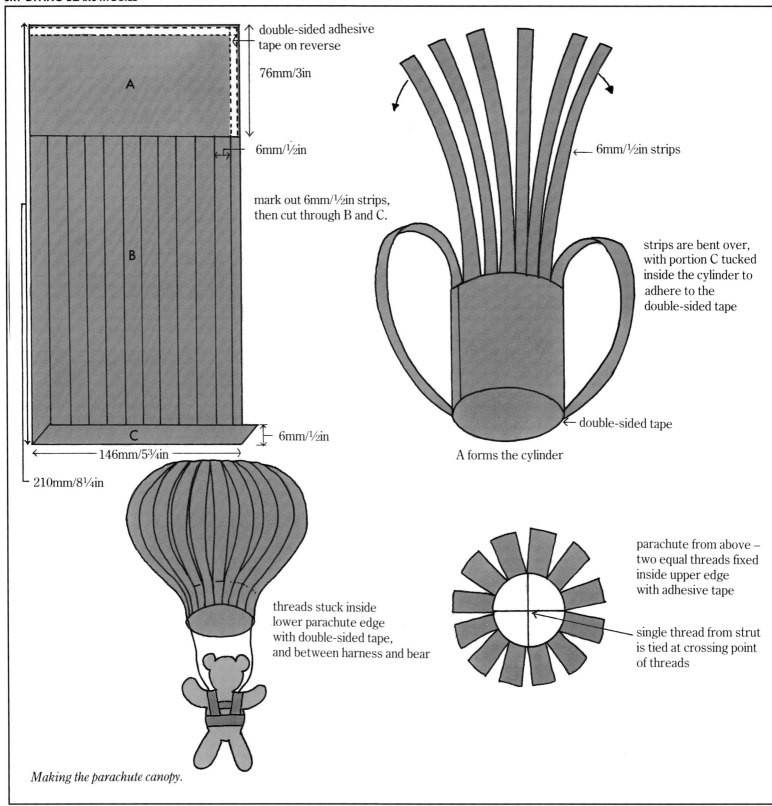

double-sided adhesive
tape on reverse

76mm/3in

6mm/½in

mark out 6mm/½in strips,
then cut through B and C.

A

B

C

6mm/½in

146mm/5¾in

210mm/8¼in

6mm/½in strips

strips are bent over,
with portion C tucked
inside the cylinder to
adhere to the
double-sided tape

double-sided tape

A forms the cylinder

threads stuck inside
lower parachute edge
with double-sided tape,
and between harness and bear

parachute from above –
two equal threads fixed
inside upper edge
with adhesive tape

single thread from strut
is tied at crossing point
of threads

Making the parachute canopy.

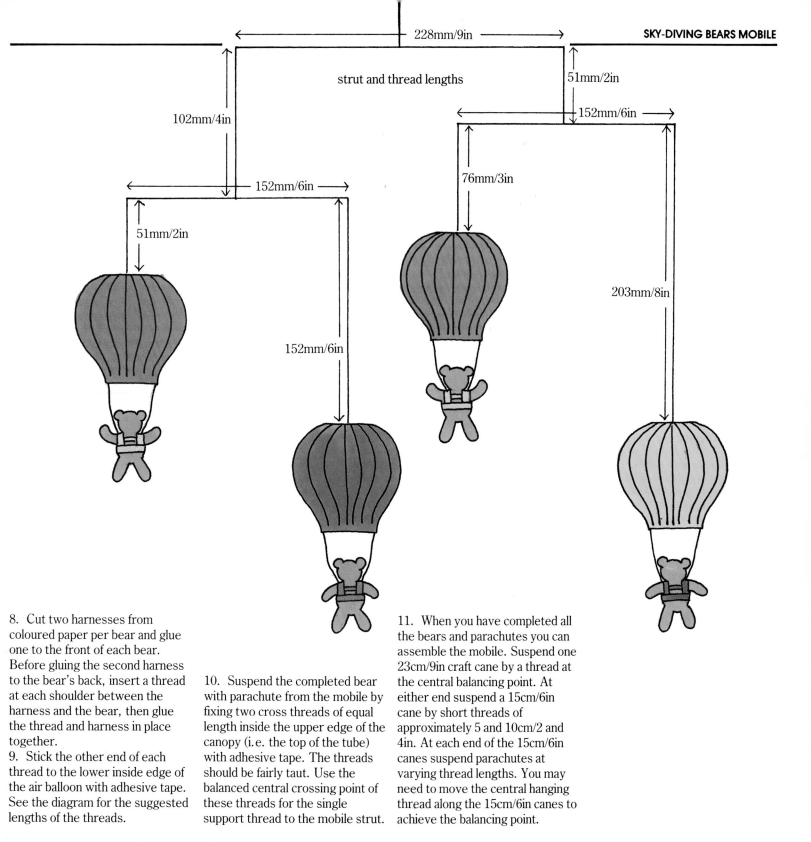

228mm/9in

strut and thread lengths

51mm/2in

102mm/4in

152mm/6in

152mm/6in

76mm/3in

51mm/2in

152mm/6in

203mm/8in

8. Cut two harnesses from coloured paper per bear and glue one to the front of each bear. Before gluing the second harness to the bear's back, insert a thread at each shoulder between the harness and the bear, then glue the thread and harness in place together.

9. Stick the other end of each thread to the lower inside edge of the air balloon with adhesive tape. See the diagram for the suggested lengths of the threads.

10. Suspend the completed bear with parachute from the mobile by fixing two cross threads of equal length inside the upper edge of the canopy (i.e. the top of the tube) with adhesive tape. The threads should be fairly taut. Use the balanced central crossing point of these threads for the single support thread to the mobile strut.

11. When you have completed all the bears and parachutes you can assemble the mobile. Suspend one 23cm/9in craft cane by a thread at the central balancing point. At either end suspend a 15cm/6in cane by short threads of approximately 5 and 10cm/2 and 4in. At each end of the 15cm/6in canes suspend parachutes at varying thread lengths. You may need to move the central hanging thread along the 15cm/6in canes to achieve the balancing point.

Teddy's Adventure Cards

98

These charming little cards, each with its own surprise element, will delight the child in us all.

Materials

A4 size thin card
Paper in suitable colours
Scissors or craft knife
Small piece of firm card
Glue
Small piece of ribbon
Hole punch

Method

1. Fold the thin A4 card in half. The two edges will form the spine of the card. Punch two holes at these edges through which to thread a small piece of ribbon to hold the card together.
2. Decide on your chosen adventure. We have illustrated the riverbank scene, which uses seven elements in the main picture, plus the surprise. On a piece of rough paper sketch out your scene to size. Keep the shapes simple, and alter their size until they fill the scene.
3. Make full cut-outs of the separate elements to fit the scene, and try them out. You could copy those given here or create your own.
4. When you are satisfied with the shapes, use them as templates to cut out the elements in coloured paper.
5. Before the final mounting of the collage, choose the site for the surprise element.
6. To make the surprise element, cut the firm card as shown and stick the feature, such as the fish, on to this. A slit should then be made in the picture base for the firm tab to slip out through. The surprise element will remain in place, as it is anchored by the wide end inside the folded sheet of card.

7. Position the slit so that when the tab is pulled it will reveal the surprise feature.
8. Finish off the card by slotting the ribbon through the holes in the card's edge and tying a neat bow. If you want the card to be free-standing, cut another piece of card the same size, punch two holes in it and fix it behind the adventure scene by slotting the ribbon through it first.

The basis for the adventure cards. ▷

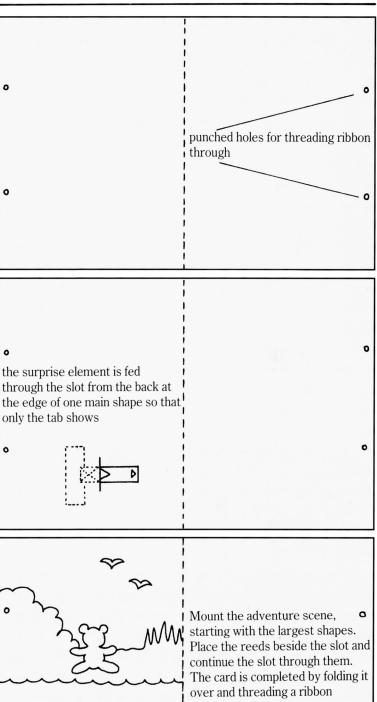

punched holes for threading ribbon through

the surprise element is fed through the slot from the back at the edge of one main shape so that only the tab shows

Mount the adventure scene, starting with the largest shapes. Place the reeds beside the slot and continue the slot through them. The card is completed by folding it over and threading a ribbon through the holes.

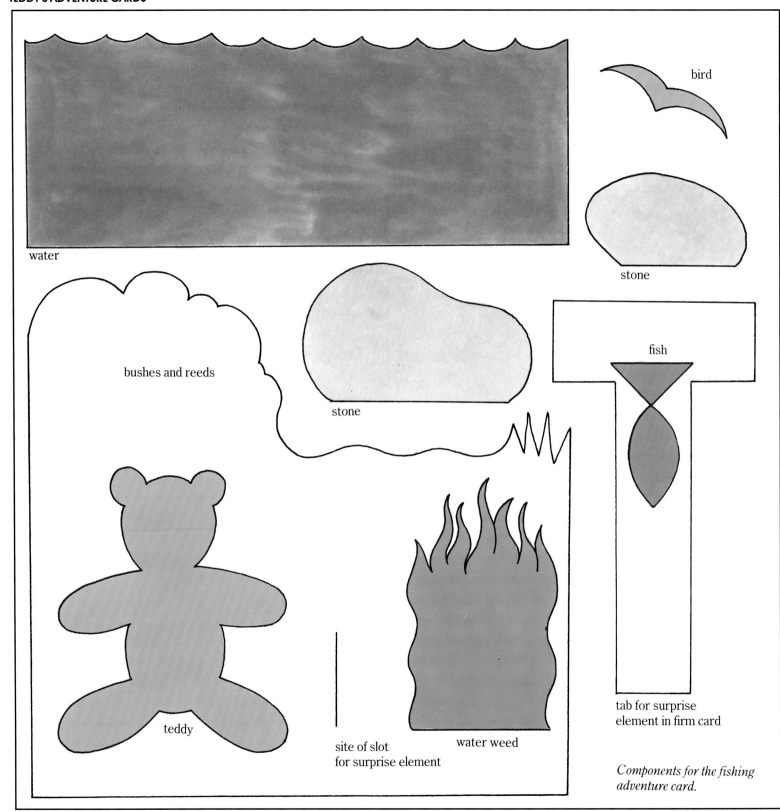

water

bird

stone

bushes and reeds

stone

fish

teddy

site of slot
for surprise element

water weed

tab for surprise
element in firm card

*Components for the fishing
adventure card.*

ducklings

rainbow days

at the fairground

'goodnight'

Surprise elements for other adventures.

Surprise features for the cards

Ducklings
One eggshell is just splitting open. Site it with the open crack upwards and the surprise element slot cut horizontally above. Make the tab an appropriate width, and mount the cut-out duckling on the tab to be pulled up and 'appear' from the eggshell.

Rainbow days
The sun appears from behind the cloud. Site the slot at the right-hand edge of the cloud. Both slot and tab need to be wide enough to accommodate a sun, which pulls out from the right.

At the fairground
Site the surprise element between two stationary roundabout horses with the pole marked above, on the tab, and below. Pull the tab upwards to make the roundabout horse move.

'Goodnight'
The slot is situated between the curtains, at the top of the window, and needs to be wide enough to accommodate the window blind. When the tab is pulled down, the blind comes down, shutting out the stars and saying 'Goodnight'.

Pop-up Birthday Teddy

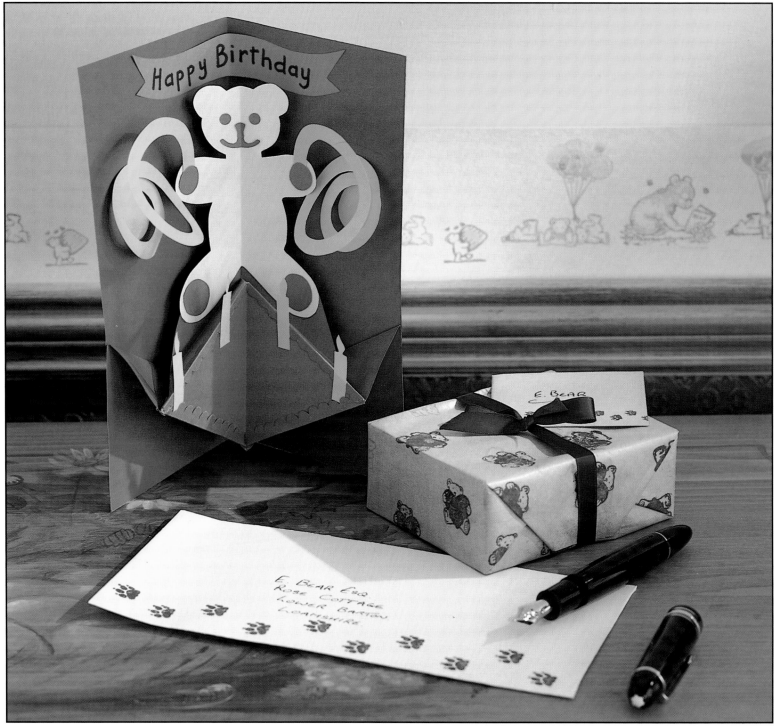

Method

This pop-up card is simple to make, yet achieves a highly professional effect.

Materials

A4 size sheets of coloured
      paper
Ruler
Glue
Double-sided adhesive tape
Scissors
Felt-tip pens, paints or
      Letraset

1. Take one A4 sheet of coloured paper and fold it in half lengthwise. Make a sharp crease.
2. Measure 19mm/¾in at the fold from the bottom of the paper and mark. Then measure 83mm/3¼in at the open edge and mark. Make a fold between these points (2a and 2b) and crease sharply.
3. Make a fold parallel to the last, 38mm/1½in further up the paper (3a and 3b).
4. From the previous fold measure 83mm/3¼in up the folded edge and mark (4a). Make a fold from this point to point 2b.

5. Make a fold parallel to the previous one, 19mm/¾in further up the paper. Open the sheet and turn it over.
6. Make a template for the teddy and draw him centrally above the diamond shape. Cut out as shown in the guideline.
7. Press all the A folds upwards, and all the B folds downwards. This enables the diagonal 'birthday cake' top to be pushed forwards, and the teddy to recede and fold backwards and downwards when the card is closed. When it is opened again, the teddy comes up and forwards. ▷

Constructing a pop-up card. ▷

A4 sheet   1a

fold 1

1b

folds 2, 3, 4, 5   1a

5a

19mm/¾in

4a

3b

5b

83mm/3¼in

2b

3a

38mm/1½in

83mm/3¼in

2a

19mm/¾in

1b

8. Once the folds are in place, flatten out the paper to add the decoration. Make a birthday teddy in your chosen colour, paint or ink on his features, and stick him on to the teddy shape. Define the cake by decorating the edges of the diamond shape with an alternative colour cut out and stuck on, to represent icing. Outline the sides and base of the cake in the same way. From another sheet of paper, cut out an appropriate number of candles and glue them on the cake.

9. The inside movement of the card is now formed. Take another piece of paper identical to the first one used and cut it down to 210mm/8¼in in height. This will make a card to fit inside a standard A4 envelope.

10. Fold this sheet lengthways down the centre. Fix the pop-up movement inside by gluing down the two lower triangles, T, only.

11. Cut the birthday streamers from a circle of coloured paper, as shown in the diagram, and position them carefully. When the card is closed, the loose end should lie just under the teddy's paw, and the circle should be perfectly flat. Fix the end of the streamer to the paw with double-sided adhesive tape, and use this or glue to fix the small centre of the circle to the backing. Thus when the card is opened and the teddy springs out, he will pull out the streamers.

12. Draw a banner shape for the top of the card, and write, paint or Letraset 'Happy Birthday' across it. Cut it out and glue it to the backing paper.

opened sheet showing pattern of folds

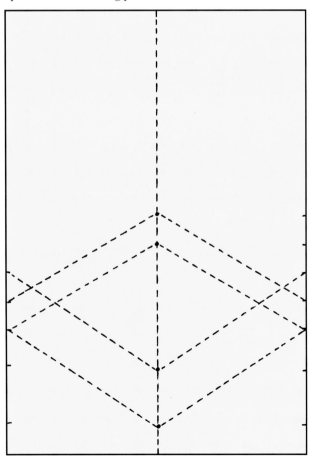

draw on teddy outline and cut out along solid line

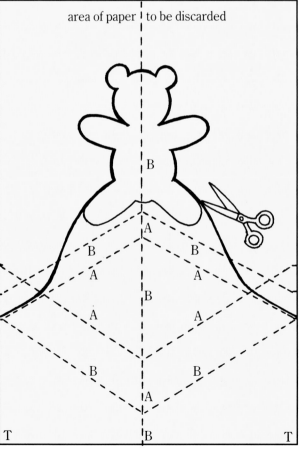

banner

candle for cake

teddy

streamer

Elements for decoration of pop-up card.

Teddy's Train

This sturdy toy is easy to make, even for the inexperienced, and gives you a choice of two carriages and two passengers.

Materials

80mm of 50 × 50mm/3¼in of 2 × 2in softwood

100mm of 25mm/4in of 1in diameter broomstick

1 metre of 5mm/1 yard of ⅕in diameter hardwood dowel

1 metre of 70 × 20mm/1 yard of 2¾ × ⅘in softwood board

500mm of 45 × 9mm/½ yard of 1¾ × ⅓in softwood lath

1 metre of 18 × 18mm/1 yard of ¾ × ¾in hardwood angle moulding

12 beechwood door knobs or wooden wheels approx. 43mm/1¾ in diameter

2 leather bootlaces or 1½ metre/1½ yard cord

Extra-fast setting wood adhesive

24 panel pins

Enamel paints

Clear wood seal

Drill

3 drill bits – diameter 1mm, 5mm and 10mm or equivalent

Fretsaw or electric skill saw

Tenon saw

Electric sander

Sandpaper

Rasp

Craft knife

Hammer

Set square

Ruler

Compass or radius-aid

Method

Engine

1. Using a tenon saw or skill saw, cut from the metre/yard length of softwood board a length measuring 150 × 70 × 20mm/6 × 2¾ × ⅘in for the baseplate. Mark 10mm/⅖in radii at each corner of the baseplate and sandpaper each corner to the radius.

2. Sand all the edges of the baseplate to a rounded shape. At the front and back of the baseplate, 10mm/⅖in from the edges and centred between the sides, drill a 5mm/⅕in hole for the towrope and coupling.

3. From the hardwood angle moulding cut two 60mm/2⅖in lengths to form the axle location brackets. Mark the axle bracket positions on the underside of the baseplate, 30mm/1⅕in from the front and back edges of the baseplate and centred between the sides.

4. With the 1mm or equivalent drill bit, drill two holes on each face of the axle brackets for the panel pins, as shown in the diagram.

5. Apply glue to the edges of the axle brackets and glue them to the baseplate, forming a V shape. Then drive four panel pins through the drilled holes into the baseplate to secure the axle brackets in position.

6. On the upper side of the baseplate mark the boiler and cab positions. The front of the boiler is placed 20mm/⅘in from the front of the baseplate; the front of the cab 100mm/4in from the front of the baseplate.

7. Mark 15mm/⅔in radii at the top of the 80 × 50 × 50mm/3¼ × 2 × 2in softwood to form the curved top of the boiler, and 12mm/½in radii at the bottom. Sandpaper the block to the marked radii, to make the rounded shape.

8. Mark the locating hole positions for the funnel and dome on the top of the boiler. The centre of the funnel hole is 20mm/⅘in from the front of the boiler; the centre of the dome hole 55mm/2⅕in. Drill 5mm/⅕in holes right through the boiler.

9. Insert a 75mm length of 5mm/3in of ⅕in of hardwood dowel in each hole and place the boiler in position on the baseplate. , Lightly tap each dowel with a hammer, which will mark the dowel positions on the baseplate.

10. Cut two lengths of broomstick, 20mm/⅘in long for the dome, and 25mm/1in long for the funnel. If the broomstick has a rounded end, use this for the dome. If not, sand it into shape.

11. Drill 5mm/⅕in holes in the bases of the funnel and dome to receive 5mm/⅕in locating dowel. Dab a small amount of wood glue on each locating dowel previously inserted in the boiler and slide the funnel and dome on to their dowels.

12. Drill 15mm/⅔in deep holes in the baseplate where the boiler locating dowels are to fit and apply glue to the underside of the boiler section and to the locating dowels. Press the boiler section down on to the baseplate, inserting each dowel into its respective hole.

13. Cut a length of board 70 × 70 × 20mm/2¾ × 2¾ × ⅘in to form the cab front. Drill two 10mm/⅖in holes for windows, each centred 15mm/⅔in from the side edges of the cab and 15mm/⅔in down from the top.

14. Cut two blocks 35mm high × 25mm wide × 20mm thick/1⅖in high × 1in wide × ⅘in thick to form the side panels of the cab. Sandpaper all the edges to a rounded shape, then glue the side panels to the cab front. Apply glue to the base of the cab and the back of the boiler section and press the cab in position behind the boiler on the baseplate.

15. Cut two lengths of 5mm/⅕in dowel, 95mm/3¾in long to form the axles for the wheels. Lightly sand the ends. Drill each wheel with the 5mm or equivalent drill at its centre. Press one wheel on to the axle, thread the axle through its locating bracket, then press the other wheel on the other end. Do not glue the wheels in place until the whole train has been completed and painted.

16. Mark the centre line of the baseplate within the cab area and drill three 5mm or equivalent holes approximately 12mm/½in deep close together to form a slot to receive the engine driver locating peg.

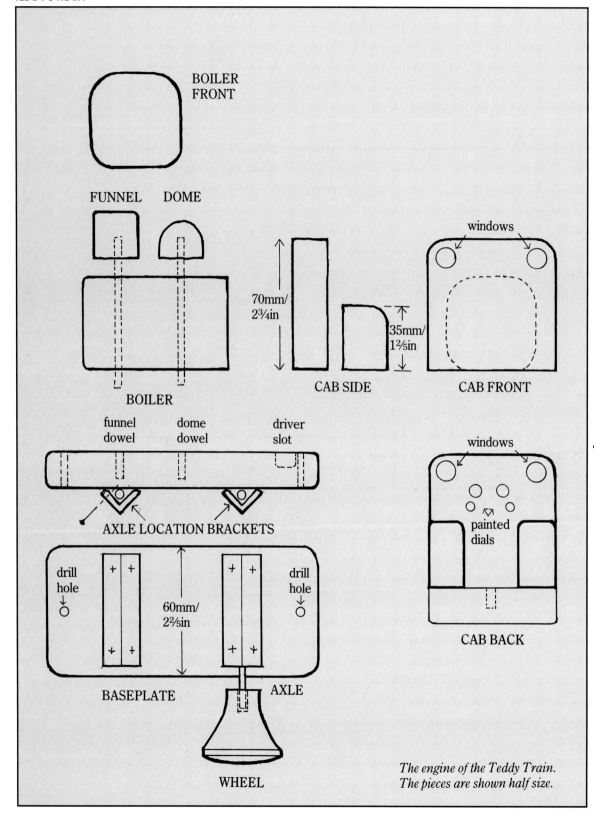

BOILER FRONT

FUNNEL   DOME

70mm/ 2¾in

BOILER

CAB SIDE

35mm/ 1⅖in

windows

CAB FRONT

funnel dowel   dome dowel   driver slot

AXLE LOCATION BRACKETS

windows

painted dials

CAB BACK

drill hole

drill hole

60mm/ 2⅖in

BASEPLATE   AXLE

WHEEL

The engine of the Teddy Train. The pieces are shown half size.

Open Wagon

1. Cut, prepare and assemble the baseplate, axle brackets, axles and wheels as for the engine, but drill the locating slot for the teddy passenger locating peg at the centre of the upper side of the baseplate.

2. Cut two 120 × 50mm/4¾ × 2in lengths (wagon sides) and two 50 × 25mm/2 × 1in lengths from the 70 × 20mm/2¾ × ⅘in softwood board. Glue the short lengths between the long lengths so as to place the sides 20mm/⅘in apart and to close the wagon body. These are the spacer blocks.

3. Sandpaper all the edges, and the tops, front and back edges to a 10mm/⅖in radius.

4. Glue the wagon body centrally to the baseplate, leaving 15mm/⅔in at each end of the baseplate and 5mm/⅕in at each side.

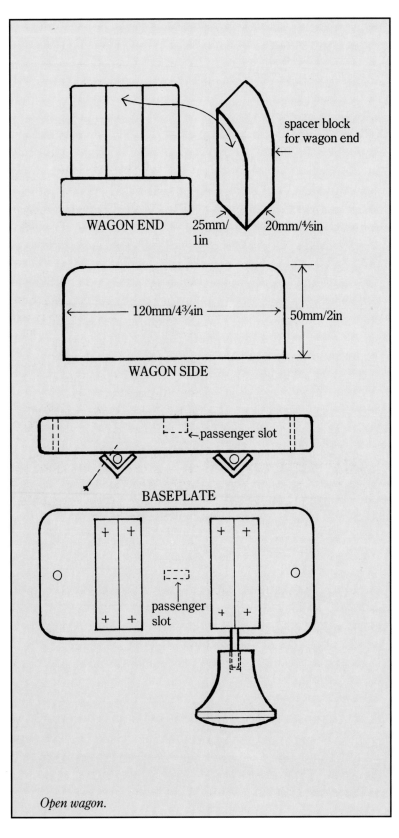

WAGON END

spacer block for wagon end

25mm/
1in   20mm/⅘in

120mm/4¾in   50mm/2in

WAGON SIDE

←passenger slot

BASEPLATE

passenger
slot

Open wagon.

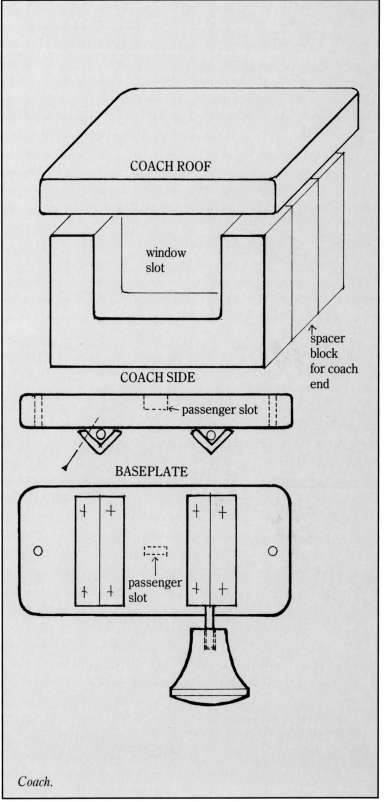

COACH ROOF

window
slot

spacer
block
for coach
end

COACH SIDE

←passenger slot

BASEPLATE

passenger
slot

Coach.

Coach

1. Cut, prepare and assemble the baseplate, axle brackets, axles and wheels as for the engine and open wagon. Make sure the teddy passenger slot is drilled and prepared at the centre of the baseplate before the closed coach body is glued on to the baseplate.
2. Cut two lengths 115 × 70 × 20mm/4½ × 2¾ × ⅘in to form the coach body sides. Set out the window sections on each side as follows: the window is 70mm/2¾in wide, positioned equidistant from both ends. Its height is 45mm/1¾in measuring from the top of the coach body. Cut out a U-shaped slot for the window and sandpaper smooth.
3. Cut one length 130 × 70 × 20mm/5 × 2¾ × ⅘in to form the coach roof. Mark 10mm/⅖in radii at each corner of the flat face and sandpaper corners to radius.
4. Cut two lengths 20 × 70 × 20mm/⅘ × 2¾ × ⅘in to fit between the coach sides and glue them to the inside faces of the coach body to close the ends of the compartment. These are the spacer blocks.
5. Glue the roof on to the coach body, equidistant about the centre lines of the body.
6. Glue the coach body to the baseplate.
7. Sandpaper all the edges and fit the axles and wheels as before.

Teddy Driver and Passengers

1. Using the diagram as a template, trace on to tracing paper and shade the reverse with a soft pencil. Place the tracing paper on the softwood lath and draw round the outline with a ballpoint pen to create an indented line on the lath.
2. Cut out the shape approximately 1mm larger than the outline with a fretsaw or electric skill saw. Sandpaper smooth.
3. Sandpaper the locating peg at the base of the teddy into a wedge shape and press the locating slot into the baseplate of the engine or rolling stock.
4. Other passengers can be created using the basic outline of the bears.

To Finish

1. Paint and seal the engine and carriages as desired. It is simplest to do the sealing first. When dry, refit the wheels and axles, gluing the wheels on to the axles.
2. Paint the teddies as desired.
3. When the paint is quite dry cut short lengths of leather bootlace or cord to make the couplings. Thread them through the holes in the front and back of the baseplate and knot.
4. Use a 750mm/30in bootlace or length of cord for the towrope at the front of the engine.

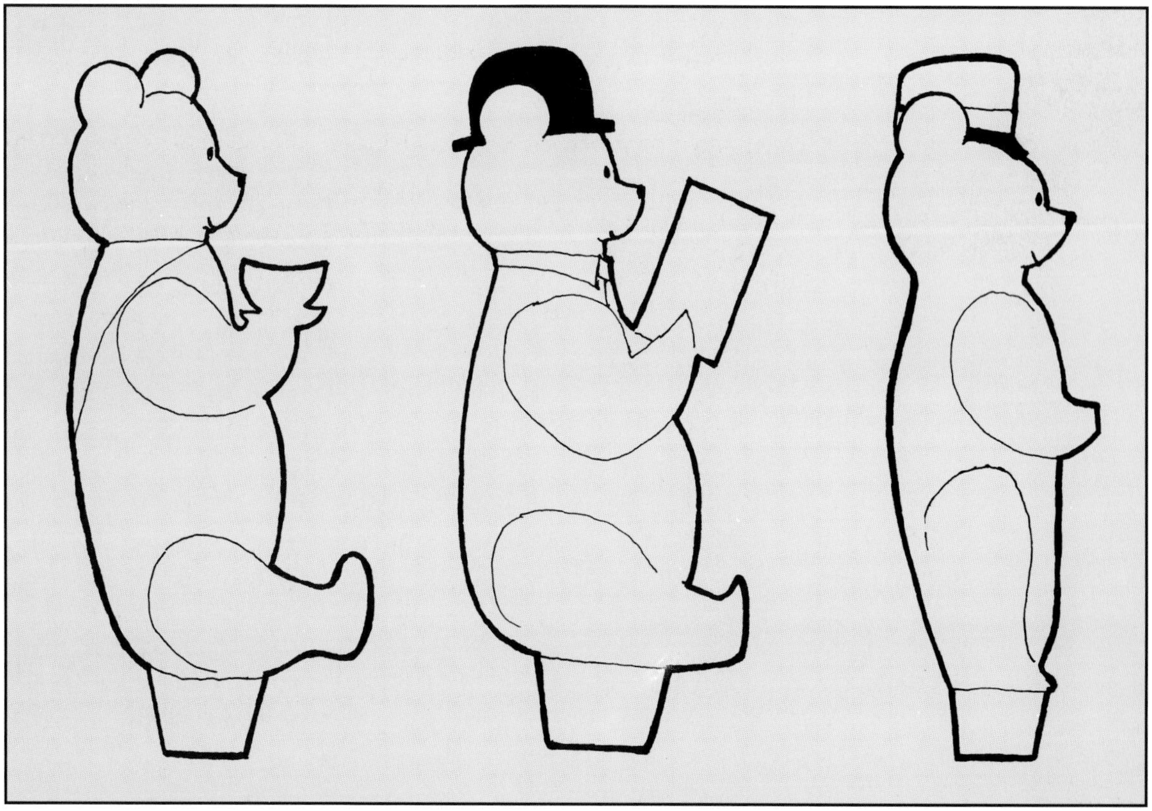

Driver (right) and passengers for the Teddy Train.

Acknowledgements

The publishers would like to thank the following people for kindly lending their materials for photography:

Antique teddy bears:
The Teddy Bear Museum,
19 Greenhill Street, Stratford-upon-Avon, Warwickshire CV37 6LF

Framed teddy bear prints:
Trevor Boult, Wendy Boult Publishing,
25 Malvern Road, Balsall Common, nr Coventry CV7 7DU

Pharao Fine Art, Seckington Cross, Winkleigh, Devon EX19 8DW

Painted furniture:
Dragons of Walton Street, 23 Walton Street, London SW3 2HX

Porcelain teddy bears:
Chessell Pottery (I.O.W.) Ltd, Yarmouth, Isle of Wight PO41 0UE

Teddy bear stamps:
First Class Stamps, The Maltings, Hall Staithe, Fakenham, Norfolk NR21 9BW

as well as:
Kathy Crump, Robert Day, Judith Lycett, Kieran Masters and Polly Pyke.